The Southern Political Tradition

Walter Lynwood Fleming Lectures in Southern History

LOUISIANA STATE UNIVERSITY

The Southern Political Tradition

MICHAEL PERMAN

LOUISIANA STATE UNIVERSITY PRESS BATON ROUGE

Published by Louisiana State University Press

Manufactured in the United States of America
FIRST PRINTING

DESIGNER: Barbara Neely Bourgoyne
TYPEFACES: Didot and Minion Pro
PRINTER: McNaughton and Gunn, Inc.
BINDER: Acme Bookbinding, Inc.

Library of Congress Cataloging-in-Publication Data

Perman, Michael.
The Southern political tradition / Michael Perman.
p. cm. — (Walter Lynwood Fleming lectures in Southern history)
Includes bibliographical references and index.
ISBN 978-0-8071-4401-5 (cloth : alk. paper) — ISBN 978-0-8071-4468-8 (pbk. : alk. paper) — ISBN 978-0-8071-4402-2 (pdf) — ISBN 978-0-8071-4403-9 (epub) — ISBN 978-0-8071-4404-6 (mobi)
1. Southern States—Politics and government. 2. Political culture—Southern States—History. I. Title.
F209.P37 2012
306.20975—dc23

2011037857

The paper in this book meets the guidelines for permanence and durability of the Committee on Production Guidelines for Book Longevity of the Council on Library Resources. ♾

Contents

Preface

The Walter Lynwood Fleming Lectures in Southern History are quite probably the longest established lecture series in the field of American history. Beginning in 1937, they have been given each year—with the exception of one year, 1942, in the middle of World War II—throughout the next seventy years before my series in 2007. The roster of lecturers is full of distinguished historians whose specialty is the American South or whose lectures deal with southern topics. So, the invitation to deliver the sixty-ninth set of lectures was a great honor and a great opportunity, but also somewhat daunting.

Whatever apprehensions I may have felt soon disappeared when I arrived in Baton Rouge to present the lectures, since I was given a generous welcome right away. My visit covered three days, and the entire experience was delightful, though admittedly very busy.

Gaines Foster, the chair of the History Department, arranged all aspects of the event and managed the visit itself with great efficiency and calm, and I want to think him especially for being such a wonderful host. I spent some time with several other faculty members, in particular Paul Paskoff, the previous History chair, but also Bill Cooper and Wayne Parent, and they too made my visit congenial as well as memorable.

A nice coda to my stay was provided through the opportunity to meet a group of seven graduate students in history on Saturday morning. We talked further about the lectures and discussed their own research interests and planned dissertation projects. And a very lively and enjoyable get-together it proved to be.

■ ■ ■

This published version of *The Southern Political Tradition* consists of the three Fleming Lectures—chapters 1, 2, and 4—and two additional chapters—3 and 5. The lectures are presented here pretty much as they were delivered. Some editorial alterations have been made, but no further material was added. The other two chapters are new. Chapter 3 takes the analysis of "The Frontier and Filibuster Defense" into its final phase during the 1940s and 1950s, with the showdown coming in July 1964 when the Civil Rights Act was passed, thereby ending legal segregation in the South, and also outlawing racial discrimination in the North. The tradition's coup de grâce came the following year when the Voting Rights Act abolished the South's system of disfranchisement. Lastly, chapter 5 provides an account of the phasing-out of the southern political tradition after 1964–65 and its replacement by an alternative system of parties and politics that is essentially similar to that in the rest of the country. But this replacement seems still to be in process and its final form not yet evident. A stable outcome may have to wait until the wild gyrations in American politics today, which produce large swings from one major party to the other in each two-year election-cycle, come to a halt.

■ ■ ■

The delay in publishing these lectures that were delivered in March 2007 is primarily due to my feeling that the three lectures did not, by themselves, constitute a book. This is something that many of my predecessors seem also to have felt. But the interval was lengthened in this case because I was already involved in one publishing project and soon became involved in another. The first was a political history of the American South that had been under contract since 2003. *Pursuit of Unity* was completed in 2009 and published early in 2010. Naturally, the ideas and topics of the lectures arose from this more general account of the course of southern politics over the past two centuries, that is, 1800–2000. The other cause of delay in composing the extra two chapters was the pressure from the new publisher to assemble a third edition of my anthology of documents and readings, *Major Problems in the Civil War and Reconstruction,* since the second edition had appeared more than a decade earlier. Once this was finished in spring 2010 (with the help, I should add, of Amy Murrell Taylor, a wonderful co-editor), I was able to get back to the writing of the new third and fifth chapters of *The Southern Political Tradition.*

Although I regret not getting the book out sooner, the extent of the delay in my case may even be near the norm. But there have been longer periods between the delivery of the lectures and the appearance of the book. The longest probably is William Leuchtenburg's publication, which took fourteen years to appear, from 1991, when the lectures were given, to 2005. But the explanation for this is that the ideas he laid down in his lectures developed into a vastly expanded and quite marvelous book, *The White House Looks South: Franklin D. Roosevelt, Harry S. Truman, Lyndon B. Johnson.* On the other hand, one set of lectures became a book about as fast as it is physically possible to make one. These were the 1978 lectures of the late Don Fehrenbacher, who, so I have been told, left his set of typed lectures, along with the completed endnotes, with the university press at the end of his visit. *The South and Three Sectional Crises,* his brilliant study of the Missouri Compromise, the Wilmot Proviso, and the Kansas Crisis, was the speedy outcome in 1980.

▪ ▪ ▪

I was, of course, very pleased that Louisiana State University Press wanted to publish my lectures. In retrospect, I am also grateful that the press did not insist on, or even suggest the need for, a deadline. Rand Dotson, the history editor, and MaryKatherine Callaway, the director, were encouraging as well as flexible, and I thank them for their continuing interest in the project during those years. Also appreciated was the very positive and thoughtful report on the manuscript from the outside reader whom the press consulted. Later on, Catherine Kadair, the senior copyeditor, became involved in this project. She gave the manuscript a careful reading that included, on a number of occasions, requests for clarification, and even several suggestions for rewriting, for all of which I am very grateful.

The Southern Political Tradition

1

The One-Party Paradigm

One of the most widely read and influential books ever written about American history is Richard Hofstadter's *The American Political Tradition and the Men Who Made It* (1948). The title of this study is derived from Hofstadter's, but the subject matter is, of course, quite different. Whereas Hofstadter described an American political tradition, my focus is on one of America's regions, the South.

At the very heart of the field of southern history is an assumption that the South has been different from the rest of the United States and that there exist characteristics and features making the region, and therefore its history, distinctive. Two of the best-known attempts to identify the essential elements of southern history are C. Vann Woodward's "The Search for Southern Identity" (1958) and Ulrich B. Phillips's "The Central Theme of Southern History" (1928).[1] This inquiry, this pursuit, has proved endlessly fascinating and elusive to historians of the American South. A check of the topics chosen for their presidential addresses by those eminences who have presided over the Southern Historical Association reveals that most of them used that very public opportunity to offer their own answer to this fundamental question. And, I might add, the temptation has frequently proved irresistible to Fleming lecturers as well.

Like the postulate of a theme or an identity, the idea of a tradition assumes that a social group, whether it be a society, a region, or a nation, develops a set of beliefs or ritual practices that then persist over a long period of time. In Hofstadter's view, America's political tradition consisted of what today we would call an ideology, a world-view. Conflicts and disagreements did arise in American political history, but they were limited and peripheral, never challenging the ideology itself. As Hofstadter defined it, this world-view upheld "the sanctity of private property, the right of the individual to dispose of and invest it, the value of opportunity, and the natural evolution of self-interest, within broad legal limits, into a beneficent social order"—in effect, a competitive and individualistic capitalist order.[2]

To demonstrate how this consensual ideology was maintained throughout the nineteenth century and into the first half of the twentieth, Hofstadter painted a series of memorable, provocative, and ironic portraits of the nation's major political leaders, seven of whom were presidents. Among those portrayed were Thomas Jefferson, "the Aristocrat as Democrat"; Andrew Jackson, agent of "the Rise of Liberal Capitalism"; John C. Calhoun, "the Marx of the Master Class"; Franklin D. Roosevelt, "the Patrician as Opportunist"; and Woodrow Wilson, "the Conservative as Liberal." In Wilson's case, Hofstadter might have further indulged his penchant for oxymoron and irony by calling the southern-born New Jersey governor and Princeton president who segregated the nation's capital, "the Southerner as Northerner." Or even vice versa!

At all events, the political biographies in *The American Political Tradition* demonstrated Hofstadter's assertion that the nation's politics was organized around the defense of a liberal variant of capitalism and that its practitioners skirmished and maneuvered, opportunistically and pragmatically, within its confines, while never countering the basic, entrenched premises of this tradition. What he perceived to be the reality of American politics did not please Hofstadter, however. He found it sterile, conservative, uninspiring, and deeply frustrating. Although his book soon became the epitome of the "consensus and continuity" school that dominated the writing of professional history in the 1950s and early 1960s, Hofstadter himself was out of step with most of this group. Unlike Daniel Boorstin and Louis Hartz, for example, he did not celebrate the political consensus he had laid bare. Instead, he deplored it.

. . .

Although my examination of the southern political tradition draws its inspiration and its title from Hofstadter's book, the approach will be rather different. This study does not consist of biographical portraits of political leaders, nor does it examine political ideas. The southern political tradition that I will describe does not emerge from the region's political *thought,* but from its political *practice.* My focus will therefore be on the political practice and behavior that seem to characterize the South. These basic elements of the region's political landscape shape how politics is conducted and carried out. Furthermore, they are not found outside the South, either in the same form or to the same degree. These essential ingredients have made the practice of politics in the South quite distinctive and, in many ways, a world unto itself.

The first of these peculiarly southern practices is the region's penchant for one-party politics. Throughout nearly two centuries of the American nation's existence—from about 1800 to the 1970s—the southern states have lived under the rule and governance of a single party. For one very brief period, however, the South enjoyed a competitive system of two parties. That was during the 1830s and 1840s, the political era often called the Second Party System, when the Democratic Party and the Whig Party came into being and began to create viable party organizations throughout the nation, including the South. But this competitive two-party politics was to prove an aberration in the South, since a system of two parties never reappeared there after the Whig Party disintegrated in the early 1850s. As Charles S. Sydnor remarked in 1948 (and he died suddenly at the age of fifty-five just hours before he was to deliver his Fleming Lectures in 1954), "The formation of the Whig party early in Jackson's second administration introduced the only thoroughgoing two-party period in all southern history."[3]

For decades after Sydnor wrote this, the South continued under one-party dominance. Eventually, beginning in the 1970s and 1980s, and certainly by the 1990s, the South embraced once again a two-party system. The impact of this latest development has implications even beyond the South. In the penultimate paragraph of their magisterial study *The Rise of Southern Republicans* (2002), Earl and Merle Black, two brothers who are the doyens of contemporary southern political science, offered this observation: "Rising congressional Republicanism in the oldest regional stronghold of the Democratic party has reshaped the Republicans into a truly national party for the first time since Reconstruction. Not since Whigs fought Democrats in the 1830s and 1840s has *American* politics been based on a thoroughly nationalized two-party system."[4] What the authors are saying, of course, is that the United States, which claims to live by, and under, the two-party system, has not been doing so for almost its entire history.

The South's experience of one-partyism can be divided into three distinct phases. The first, from 1800 until 1860, can be characterized as the period of "one-party dominance," in which all but those two anomalous decades of the 1830s and 1840s witnessed the ascendancy first of the Jeffersonian Republicans and then of the Jacksonian Democrats. A brief interlude followed during the Confederacy, 1861–1865, when the seceded South experimented with no parties at all. In the forty years after the Civil War, the region was subjected to a regime in which one party, the Democrats, refused to accord legitimacy to their Republican opponents. They thereby removed an ingredient that is essential to a viable two-party, or even a multi-party, system—namely, the legitimacy and right to participate and govern of both, or all, parties that are protagonists within the polity. This phase, from the 1870s up to about 1908, may aptly be categorized as the period of "one-party hegemony." And finally, the third phase was a qualitatively different regime from its predecessors. Usually described as the "Solid South," this was nothing less than a "one-party system." It became institutionalized after the Republican opposition was decimated and all but eliminated at the turn of the twentieth century. No opposition party was allowed to emerge after the rules of the game were officially and formally rewritten as a result of the revision of their constitutions by the southern states between 1890 and 1908. This one-party system soon became entrenched, and it lasted until the 1960s, when it was dismantled and, over the next three decades, was gradually replaced by the seemingly viable two-party politics of Democrats and Republicans of today.

THE ERA OF ONE-PARTY DOMINANCE, 1800–1860

From the very beginning, when political parties first emerged just a few years after the founding of the new nation, one of them was distinctly southern in its origins and management. The Republican Party, as it was generally known, was founded by two prominent Virginians, Thomas Jefferson and James Madison. Both men, but Madison in particular, had endorsed the new federal constitution. Nevertheless, both were soon appalled by the direction in which the secretary of the treasury, Alexander Hamilton, was taking the infant nation at its most formative moment. Hamilton's grand design envisaged the central government as the coordinator of the nation's financial and fiscal system and the engine behind its economic development. Because the model for Hamilton's plan was avowedly the finance-driven, centralized governmental system of Great Britain and because the main beneficiaries of America's version of it would undoubtedly be the commercial interests in the northeastern states, the two Virginians were convinced that this was not the appropriate path for Britain's former colony, and in particular the overwhelmingly agricultural southern part of it

Hamilton's scheme was overly bold and extreme, and it favored just a few economic interests to the exclusion of the rest. Since most of the country was either indifferent or actively hostile, rallying opposition to the program that soon became identified with the Federalist Party was not difficult. All it required was an oppositional stance, with little need to formulate alternative proposals. To this end, the Republicans insisted that the central government be limited ("wise and frugal" was how Jefferson depicted it in his First Inaugural Address); that the states function as a counterweight to federal overreaching; and that the republic's economy develop naturally and gradually, without artificial government stimulation and along mainly agricultural lines.

This negative stance was sufficiently broad and unspecific to rally massive support. In the South, it made the Republican Party unassailable. In the 1796 presidential election, John Adams, the Federalist, won just two electoral votes there, while a mere five of the forty-five congressional seats in the region were carried by the Federalists in the mid-to-late 1790s. In 1800, when Jefferson himself ran for the presidency, he won 85 percent of the southern states' electoral vote. Four years later, Jefferson won every southern electoral vote except for a few in North Carolina, while the Federalists held just a couple of congressional seats and failed even to contest forty others in Virginia, the Carolinas, and Georgia. At this point, the historian of the southern Federalists, James Broussard, had to acknowledge that, "as an effective opposition," the Federalist Party was finished.[5]

Over the next few decades, the Federalist Party proved incapable of expanding beyond its narrow base in port cities like Charleston and Wilmington and in urban commercial areas, such as Fayetteville in North Carolina, Richmond in Virginia, and Savannah and Augusta in Georgia. At the same time, the South's Republicans were establishing a lockhold on the presidency by means of the nominating system created by the party in Virginia. Deploying its influence as the region's most populous state and using its ability through what was known as the "general ticket" system to cast its electoral votes as a unit, Virginia managed to determine the Republican Party's nominee and secure his election. At the head of this process was a central committee called the Richmond Junto. The Junto's task was to coordinate and maximize the state's capacity to control the nomination at the party caucus in Congress and to mobilize the party's voters at the general election in the southern states themselves. The result was the Virginia Dynasty of three consecutive two-term presidents—Jefferson, Madison, and Monroe—from 1800 to 1824. Remarkably, this highly centralized mechanism for controlling the presidency was forged by Republicans in the South, where party organization was less developed than in any other part of the country. The reason for this was simple: party organization was virtually unnecessary because Federalist opposition to the Republicans had been so marginal and ineffectual from the outset.

From the late 1790s until 1824, the South was therefore solidly Republican. And this one-party dominance would continue until the early 1830s, when a new party arose to promote the presidential candidacy of Andrew Jackson. The Democratic Party was conceived principally as an electoral organization to put the Tennessee slaveholder and Indian fighter in the White House. His first bid in 1824 had been foiled by two Washington insiders, John Quincy Adams and Henry Clay, who had schemed to keep the outsider where he belonged—outside, and safely out of power. But the party's formation had two other purposes, and these were visionary. First, Jefferson's Republican Party had strayed from its minimalist, oppositional origins and was currently absorbing some of the programmatic, centralizing policies previously dismissed as Hamiltonian. Renaming the party as the National Republicans, its leadership, now typified by Adams and Clay, was espousing such heresies as a national bank, a protective tariff, and also federally sponsored internal improvement projects intended to build the new nation's transportation infrastructure. It was time, then, to challenge this so-called "American system" with a new party based on the original Jeffersonian agenda and principles.

The new party's second purpose was to function as a bridge connecting the two parts of the country, increasingly designated as the North and the South, that seemed to be pulling apart from each other and threatening the nation's unity. In 1819–21, the Missouri Crisis had sounded the alarm that differences between free and slave states were percolating to the surface of American politics. The architect of this new political party was New York's Martin Van Buren, Jackson's leading organizer in the North. He believed that a revitalization of the earlier Jeffersonian alliance between "the planters of the South and the plain republicans of the North," that is, its laborers and farmers, was essential to offset and suppress the sectional animosities over slavery that were assuming dangerous proportions.[6] The national party that Van Buren envisaged was expected to suppress, or at least tamp down, sectional antipathies. Thomas Ritchie, editor of the *Richmond Enquirer* and head of the Richmond Junto, and John C. Calhoun, secretary of war under Monroe and now vice-president in the Adams administration, were the leading southerners to whom Van Buren appealed for support as he reorganized the old Jeffersonian Republican Party into the new Jacksonian Democrats.

The upshot of these plans and negotiations was the formation of the Democratic Party that carried Jackson to victory in 1828. The party was intended to be national, and it did in fact do well throughout the country. But the Tennessean's support in the South was massive. He carried every southern state's entire electoral vote except Maryland's, which split six to five for Adams. In the popular vote, Jackson was supported almost unanimously in Tennessee, Georgia, Alabama and Mississippi, while North Carolina and Virginia went overwhelmingly for him. Even Clay's Kentucky ended up in the Jackson column. When he ran for reelection in 1832, Old Hickory again swept the South with huge majorities, ranging from 75 percent in Virginia to just under 100 percent in Georgia and Mississippi. Outside Kentucky, Maryland, and Louisiana, he carried all but a dozen counties in the southern states.[7] The South was again solidly in one party, but it was Jackson Democratic now, rather than Jefferson Republican.

During the next decade and a half, from the mid-1830s to the early 1850s, the dominance of the Jacksonian Democrats was challenged in the South by a revitalized and reorganized National Republican Party, which began to call itself the Whig Party. Originating in Congress as a visceral reaction to "executive usurpation" on the part of King Andrew the First, the Whigs coalesced behind the leadership of Henry Clay and his program of federally sponsored economic development, a somewhat altered and reduced version of a grander scheme espoused earlier by President John Quincy Adams. Support for the Whigs emerged within the South initially in opposition to Jackson's growing high-handedness in his use of presidential power. But that southern support for the Whigs continued to grow, for two reasons. First, because Jackson threatened to put down the South Carolina nullifiers who refused to pay the high rates of the 1828 tariff on imported goods. And second, because Old Hickory arranged for his northern vice-president, Martin Van Buren, to succeed him in 1836. The final straw was the economic Panic of 1837 for which President Van Buren seemed to offer no effective remedy, while the Whigs seemed to be the party with economic plans and answers. In 1840 the Whigs won the presidency after managing to establish a viable presence in most of the southern states.

In the decade of the 1840s, the South underwent what was, and would become, an unfamiliar experience—an encounter with two competitive political parties. The Whigs were particularly strong in those urban, commercial areas where the Federalists had been viable. But they were also preferred by the wealthy, and the well-to-do in general, who were worried by Jackson's hostility to banks and by the turmoil that his economic policies generated, leading to the Panic of 1837. Thus, Jackson's attack on the "Money Power" and his identification with the "common man" and the masses further alienated the southern gentry.

Many of these members of the region's economic and social elite were not in fact bankers and merchants but slaveholding planters and large farmers, and they too fell in behind the Whigs in sufficient numbers to make the party a viable political force. In four southern states in particular—five if Kentucky is included—the Whigs actually presented a serious challenge to the Democrats. Three were the Upper South states of Virginia, North Carolina, and Tennessee, where the mountain regions found themselves in need of economic development through the building of transportation links and other infrastructure that the Tidewater planters who were all Democrats refused to provide. Naturally, the Whigs, who were advocates of development at the national level, could be relied upon to remedy these deficiencies. And the Whigs also benefited from the preexistent struggle for political influence within these states between the underdeveloped up-country and the unresponsive low country. Also strongly pro-Whig were two states where powerful economic interests needed tariff protection, the hemp growers of Kentucky and the sugar industry in Louisiana. Also providing additional strength to the Whigs in Louisiana was the commercial elite of New Orleans.

The resultant two-party rivalry was at its height in the 1840s. But the Whigs soon went into a terminal decline, while the Democrats encountered difficulties trying to hold their national party together. Paradoxically, the cause of this destabilization of the national party system was its inability to suppress the sectional antipathy that was one of the primary reasons for developing national parties in the first place. The sections became so salient in the 1840s that the national parties, despite their efforts, were unable to counteract or stifle the differences between North and South, as Van Buren had hoped they might.

This intensifying sectionalism was stimulated primarily by the emergence in the 1830s of an uncompromising, radical movement to abolish slavery. Over the next decade, abolitionist propaganda and protest increased, while also giving rise to a broad sentiment outside the South that was hostile to slavery, though rarely demanding that slavery be abolished. In response, an intensifying pressure from within the South arose, insisting on national recognition of—and by the 1850s, even protection for—slavery, which was the economic interest as well as the racial institution that had come to define the southern region.

Rather than deflecting the issue from the southern states where slavery already existed, the territorial expansion resulting from the annexation of Texas in 1845 and the war against Mexico of 1846–48 presented a problem requiring immediate solution. And it destroyed the Whigs, while splitting the Democrats deeply along sectional lines. In the South, the sudden collapse of the Whig Party between 1852 and 1854 was followed by five or six years of drift, as the opposition to the Democrats tried to find alternative party vehicles. First, they looked to the American Party that had sprung up very suddenly in the North as an anti-immigrant, anti-Catholic organization. Unfortunately the Know-Nothings, as this new party's members were stigmatized by their opponents, turned out to be anti-slavery as well, just like the northern Whigs. At this point, the opponents of the Democrats formed coalitions consisting of former Whigs and former Know-Nothings, invariably calling themselves the "Opposition." But these alliances failed to cohere or to offer a serious challenge to the Democrats. In effect, the South had reverted to form and had become once again a one-party region.

In 1861, the southern states seceded from the Union and formed an independent country. The politics of this embryonic nation would not assume the one-party form, however. Instead, the Confederacy broke new ground. Or, more accurately perhaps, it returned to the 1780s and the intentions of the framers of the United States governmental system, who had no use for political parties in a republic. For the Confederates inaugurated a politics without parties—in other words, a no-party system. This was actually what John C. Calhoun had wanted for the South in the 1830s and 1840s. He had sought a united South unattached to the two major parties, the Whigs and Democrats. The resulting sectional party would be a cohesive and unaligned political entity, so Calhoun assumed, and it would operate as a balance-wheel between the other two parties, throwing its support to whichever one was more sympathetic, or alternatively, withholding support altogether from one or the other of them. Of course, this maneuver was conceived as a way of protecting the South within the Union. In all likelihood, however, Calhoun would have recommended such a system for the Confederacy, since he detested parties and wanted to return to the pre-Jacksonian Era of Good Feelings when mass-based party organizations, bestowing the spoils of office on their grateful and subservient supporters, did not exist.

To this end, the incoming president of the Confederacy, Jefferson Davis, saw himself as a "patriot president," who, like Washington, stood above party and faction. And the Confederate constitution established a six-year, nonrenewable term so that a president would not have to run again and therefore would not need to form an electoral organization, or party, to help him round up votes. The constitution also included a number of devices to discourage, if not suppress, political parties. The president's power over appointments was limited by prohibiting him from removing officials below the cabinet level except for cause, thereby denying him the main source of executive patronage that had become the breeding ground for permanent political parties in Jackson's time. Further barriers to the emergence of a "spoils system" in the Confederacy were stipulations strictly prohibiting Congress from enacting protective tariffs or promoting schemes of internal improvement—both of them federal programs that southerners had opposed vehemently and successfully in the 1830s.

The Confederates' aversion to political parties was also evident in the political system they created. Previous party allegiance (Whig or Democrat) or stand on secession (immediate secession or reluctant cooperationism) could have formed the basis for parties in the new Confederacy. But the possibility was denounced by President Davis, a secessionist himself. He organized his cabinet according to states, giving one office to a representative from each state. Meanwhile, his vice-president, Alexander H. Stephens, a cooperationist from Georgia, warned a large audience in Savannah on 21 March 1861, "If we become divided—if schisms arise—if dissensions spring up—if factions are engendered—if party spirit, nourished by unholy personal ambition shall rear its hydra head, I have no good prophesy for you."[8]

In the first Confederate elections, in November 1861, the Davis-Stephens ticket and the constitution were merely ratified with little opposition. At the congressional level, candidates ran as individuals, not as candidates of any party. Two years later, elections to the Confederate Congress were again conducted in similar fashion, with none of the party caucuses and conventions, none of the electioneering and hoopla, of mass party politics. Accordingly, turnout was low and election day eerily quiet. Supplementing this partyless electoral system was the lack of party organization and structure inside the Confederate Congress itself. Members who had been elected as individuals functioned in the same way once they debated and voted in Congress. "Lawmaking was every man for himself, for Congress was an amorphous body in which it seemed that almost every atom behaved according to its own rules."[9] This was the conclusion of Thomas B. Alexander and Richard E. Beringer, the historians of the Congress, who discovered that Davis never created any semblance of an administration party to promote his own policies. Meanwhile, his opponents were totally unorganized. Not even a group of a half-dozen or so known Davis-haters ever got together to coordinate their angry, contemptuous opposition and then maintain this cohesion, and maybe even expand it, over the course of several votes. Yet this lamentable situation was rarely, if ever, denounced or criticized. Rather, it was welcomed as evidence that parties and "party spirit" had been banished from the Confederacy's model republic, just as the creators of the U.S. governmental system had originally intended in the 1780s.

During the decade or so following the defeat of the Confederacy, the South's political world was transformed. After several years of bitter, though ultimately ineffective, resistance against the terms for readmission to the Union proposed first by President Andrew Johnson and then by the Republican-controlled Congress, the former Confederates were confronted by a mandatory plan for reunion and readmission known as the Reconstruction Act, passed in March 1867. Under the terms of this statute, a new political system was introduced into the South. The political and military leaders of the Confederacy were disfranchised and also disqualified from holding office. African Americans, whether free blacks or freed slaves, were enfranchised. And a branch of the Republican Party was formed in the South that, as a result of the elections held in 1868, assumed control of the region's state governments. At the same time, the South's delegation in Congress became entirely Republican.

State power had been taken from the South's political and economic elite and transferred to a political party that embodied Congress's Reconstruction policy. Its aim was to move the region in a new direction, with free labor, equal rights, activist government, and economic development as the main ingredients.

THE ERA OF ONE-PARTY HEGEMONY, 1868–1908

Even before the 1868 elections, the issue had been joined, however. White southerners "are not *ruled* by any government they do not recognize as legitimate over them," the *Charleston Mercury* threatened. "The white race of the South have only to will the rule of the South, and there is no power on this continent, which can prevent it."[10] Imposed from outside the region by its northern Republican enemies and led and supported within the South by social elements that were deemed unsouthern, the ascendant Republican Party was a usurper, devoid of legitimacy and deserving neither respect nor obedience.

From the outset, the party's pretensions and competence were assailed by the anti-Reconstruction press, consisting of the powerful, traditional newspapers of the region such as the *Charleston Mercury*, the *Jackson Clarion*, the *Raleigh Sentinel*, and the *Montgomery Advertiser*. And ridicule and derision were the weapons they employed. Because the conventions that wrote the required new constitutions in 1867–68 contained black delegates, they were scorned as "mongrel menageries" filled with "baboons, monkeys, mules . . . and other jackasses."[11] Of course, the northerners who joined the Republican Party were derided as men of no account, mere itinerant "carpetbaggers," while the native southerners who affiliated with the party, and therefore betrayed their homeland and their race, were dismissed as "scalawags."

Denouncing these Republican governments as ludicrous and contemptible was merely a preliminary to the real work at hand, the destabilization and eventual overthrow of the alien Reconstruction regime.

The northern Republican congressmen who devised the Reconstruction Act anticipated the emergence of serious opposition to the new party they were creating in the postwar South. Nevertheless, they hoped that the newly formed southern Republican Party would be able to exploit its control of southern state government and thereby manage to build up the party and expand its base of support. Commercial interests and railroad promoters who wanted a "New South" as well as the many white farmers and laborers who desperately needed a new deal could well become the basis of a viable and enduring southern Republican Party. If the party could develop support from these groups, it would become established and be able to mount strong election campaigns against its Democratic opponents within a normalized political environment of two-party competition. This outcome was quite possible in 1868 and 1869, because many leading Democrats believed they could win over southern whites and regain control at the ballot box by electoral means. But other Democrats were declaring openly that the Republicans were illegitimate and unsouthern and therefore had to be removed, and this sentiment was widespread and intimidating. Indeed, this rigid, confrontational stance soon forestalled the emergence of normal, competitive electoral politics.

Destabilization of the illegitimate Republican administrations was evident in the way their Democratic opponents treated them. In the first place, the Republican Party was viewed as an organization that should not just be defeated through the electoral process, but must be undermined and broken up. Democrats were relentless in their schemes to encourage dissidence within the Republican Party that would result in discontented factions bolting and running as third-party independents or, even better, allying with the Democrats themselves. And in the black-majority districts, Democrats worked with shameless cynicism to cut deals with black Republicans to share the offices through joint "fusion" tickets and coalitions. Even more threatening and damaging to the Republicans was the Democrats' resort to violence in order to intimidate the new party's voters and silence its leaders. These attacks took myriad forms—from physical attacks on individual voters, either before an election or on their way home after voting, to assassinations of party leaders. This pattern of violence began as early as 1868 during the first campaigns waged by the Republicans.

Between 1868 and 1871, the emergence of the hooded and armed Ku Klux Klan organization destabilized the Republicans in a number of states. Although the Democrats themselves did not create the Klan, they clearly approved of it and encouraged it, since its objectives were primarily political. Moreover, it was most active in the up-country areas of most states, where the balance of white and black populations was so close that violence against a small but crucial group of Republicans could swing a state to the Democrats. In upstate South Carolina in September 1870, the state's chief constable reported to the Republican governor that "a complete organization exists from the Savannah river to Chester, a distance of nearly two-hundred miles in length, and that its object is to intimidate Republican voters on Election Day and if necessary murder leading Republicans."[12] The upshot of the Klan's activities and of the Democrats' fomentation of divisions within the Republicans' ranks was weakened Republican parties and destabilized Republican governments. As a result, the party lost control of five states between 1870 and 1874.

Partly as a result of federal military and judicial intervention in 1871–72, the Klan was effectively disbanded. Nevertheless, organized violence reemerged several years later in the Lower South states that were still under Republican control. This time, the Democratic Party mobilized paramilitary formations, such as the Rifle Clubs in Mississippi and the Red Shirts in South Carolina, which terrorized black districts prior to the state elections of 1875 and 1876 respectively. Or like the White Leagues in Louisiana that, in the mid-1870s, mounted military assaults on a number of parish governments (Louisiana's counties are called parishes) under Republican control. By means of election campaigns that rallied their supporters around the need to maintain white supremacy and that relied on the use of violence and intimidation against the Republicans' black voters, the Democrats succeeded in defeating the last remaining Republican governments in the Lower South. Although this victory was achieved through elections, the reality of the Democrats' campaigns was the undermining of Republican control and driving off its supporters by whatever means necessary. This was not a normal electoral competition between two political parties, but an all-out contest for control by the party that considered itself alone to be legitimate and qualified to govern. With the overthrow of the Republicans (and people at the time as well as historians later have applied the term *overthrow* to describe the process at work here), the Reconstruction regime of the Republicans was replaced by the Redemption regime of the Democrats. This was not just the normal transfer of power after an election from one political party to another. It was regime change.

By 1877, the hegemony sought by the Democrats, who considered themselves the South's only legitimate party, had been seized and secured. The next thirty years witnessed the steady consolidation of this new one-party regime. The process occurred in two stages. In the first, during the 1880s, the Democrats who had, as they put it, "redeemed the South from Radical Misrule" organized their broad coalition around a commitment to inactive government and minimal taxes and expenditures. The party's priorities were typified by the proud boast of George F. Drew, Florida's governor in the late 1880s: "Spend nothing unless absolutely necessary."[13] Binding the Democrats together even more tightly was their identity as "the white man's party," the party of white supremacy. Whenever any challenge arose, whether from the Republicans or from any new reform party like the Greenback Party or the Readjuster Party in Virginia in the early 1880s, the charge was unleashed that its existence threatened white unity and supremacy. Invariably, that scare proved sufficient to damn the opposition and keep Democratic ranks firm.

The hegemony of the Democrats also rested on their ability to restrict and repress the black vote, through the manipulation of both the system of elections (which they controlled) and the balloting process on election day itself. By means of intimidation and electoral fraud, the

Democrats denied their opponents, the Republicans in particular, the vote of African Americans upon which they relied, while they stuffed Democratic ballot boxes with black votes in black-majority districts, where the white man's party was naturally in the minority. Systematic electoral fraud like this was justified if it guaranteed the hegemony of the white man's party that had delivered the region from "the horrors of Reconstruction."

THE ERA OF THE ONE-PARTY SYSTEM, 1908–1960S

The second phase in the consolidation of the one-party regime took place during the 1890s and into the first decade of the twentieth century. After manipulating and suppressing the black vote, a political activity that was proving to be tiresome and awkward, and not always effective, the Democrats decided to settle the matter once and for all by simply eliminating the black vote altogether.

State by state, beginning with Tennessee and Mississippi in 1890, the Democrats mounted campaigns to amend or rewrite the region's state constitutions so as to exclude all African Americans. Constitutional revision was a complicated and lengthy procedure that could, at any point, go awry if significant opposition arose. Even more threatening was a known obstacle, the Fifteenth Amendment, that had federalized the right to vote during Reconstruction and prohibited its denial on the grounds of race. Yet the disfranchisers were proudly and shamelessly avowing that the purpose of their movement was to get rid of the black vote. As Solomon S. Calhoon, the president of the Mississippi constitutional convention, told the delegates in his opening address: "Let us tell the truth if it bursts the bottom of the Universe. We came here to exclude the negro. Nothing short of this will answer."[14] Faced with the constitutional amendment, their only recourse was to execute an end-run around it. And so they based the new suffrage qualifications on nonracial categories, such as literacy, residence, and the payment of taxes. Since many poor and illiterate whites would be disqualified by provisions like these, the party of white supremacy created loopholes to "let in" large numbers of whites who were otherwise ineligible members of the superior race. These were the notorious "grandfather" and "understanding" clauses.

By 1908, the former Confederate states had disfranchised all but a few thousand of each state's black voters. In addition, more than a million white voters throughout the region probably lost the vote because, so it appeared, they were unwilling to apply for special treatment under the loophole clause of their state's new constitution. The results were devastating, as the registered electorate plummeted to less than a third of the previously eligible adult male population. This small electorate contained no blacks and very few poor and illiterate whites. Also eliminated from politics was the opposition. Deprived of its African American base, the Republican Party was reduced to a remnant, except in the mountains of east Tennessee and in the western parts of Virginia and North Carolina. Also shattered were the Populists, whose emergence as a result of the agricultural crisis of the 1890s had frightened the Democrats and prompted them to vow "never again" to permit serious opposition to exist in the region.

Some of these consequences had not been intended by the disfranchisers' campaigns. One result of their assault on democracy had certainly not been planned, and that was the redundancy of the general election. Elimination of most of the voters seemed to the "capital D" Democratic disfranchisers to be an acceptable deficiency in a "small d" democratic system. But the elimination of contested elections as well caused them some concern. They therefore seized on the idea, currently being proposed by Progressive reformers in the North, of a primary election to choose a party's nominees and candidates. The primary would make it possible to retain election contests. But it would also ensure that the Democrats, who were now the sole party in the South, could avoid splits and independent candidacies by seekers of their party's nomination who had failed in the attempt and vowed to run on their own in the general election. (That is, they wanted to avoid what Joseph Lieberman did in the Senate race in Connecticut in November 2006, when he ran in the election against his own party's nominee. As a result, the Democrat lost the election to Lieberman, who ran as an independent.) Having made elections between political parties virtually irrelevant, the South's Democrats created a replacement in the form of an election for their party's nominee, who would almost certainly go on to win the general election against minimal Republican opposition. And just to make sure that blacks could not reenter the political system by claiming to be eligible to vote in internal party primary elections as opposed to general elections, these primaries were to be categorized as racially exclusive "white primaries." After claiming for the previous forty years that they were the only legitimate political party in the South, the Democrats had now removed the last traces of Reconstruction and secured the unchallenged hegemony—in effect, the monopoly—they believed was rightfully theirs.[15]

This permanent ascendancy had been achieved by dispensing with the essential features of a modern system of representative democracy, namely, universal suffrage and viable, competitive political parties. In the process of attaining this supremacy, the Democrats had actually, though perhaps unwittingly, created a new political system. For the formal institutions were in place for a one-party system that would continue in existence with little or no change for more than half a century. If southern politics in the nineteenth century can be categorized as one-party dominance followed by one-party hegemony, then for most of the twentieth, it was a one-party system. In the nineteenth century, the political system *allowed* for several parties but, except for the 1830s and 1840s, generated only one. In the twentieth century until the 1970s, the system was *intended* to produce and sustain just one party. And, not surprisingly, it always did so.

The South's one-party system was constructed out of three elements: a severely restricted electorate of specially qualified white voters; a marginalized, almost nonexistent, opposition party; and a whites-only primary election for choosing the Democratic nominee, who would be certain to win the general election. Even though this structure had been erected in order to maintain a monopoly on political activity and power in the South, the Democratic Party, which was the beneficiary and embodiment of this monopoly, was not the formidable political organization one might have imagined. In actual fact, it was a quite feeble institution. Because the only real election was the primary to choose its candidates, the party had no need to forge an electoral apparatus to mobilize its supporters and get them to the polls in order to counter an aroused partisan enemy. So its electoral machinery atrophied. As a result, the main activity and justification of American political parties—which is to operate as electoral organizations, or machines, to get out the vote—no longer applied to the Democratic Party in the South. Furthermore, the party was only minimally involved in its own primaries. Candidates announced quite independently of the party organization and then ran and financed their own campaigns. The party paid only for administering primary elections, mainly appointing election judges and providing the ballots and ballot boxes, while the state or local government was responsible for the cost of the general elections. As V. O. Key acknowledged in his authoritative *Southern Politics in State and Nation* (1949), the Democratic Party functioned as little more than "an agency to administer elections, since it has to fight no campaigns."[16]

Instead of a vital, highly organized electoral machine, the southern Democratic Party was a shell of a political party. It provided an arena within which political aspirants ran for nomination, but it possessed few other functions. And certainly, there were no major responsibilities and objectives for which it had to energize its members and supporters or coordinate and direct its organization. As a result, the Democratic Party degenerated into loose factions and groupings, while the primary system encouraged a politics of personality as individuals sought to draw attention to themselves and differentiate themselves from their rivals. To Key, these developments produced a "disorganized politics" which, the more he examined it, the more deficient and inadequate he found it.

Eventually, he derided it as an "atomized," a "pulverized," politics. With the only existing political party functioning merely as "a holding company for competing factions," the South's one-party system might even be described with accuracy as a no-party system. Indeed, Key concluded that "the South, unlike most of the rest of the democratic world, really has no political parties."[17]

V. O. Key's observation is most puzzling. At first sight, it seems counterintuitive, even wrong-headed. How could a weak and unorganized political party emerge as the outcome of a formal political structure reared for the sole purpose of making that party supreme and unassailable? Almost without exception, one-party systems are dominated, even controlled, by a single unquestionably powerful, even all-powerful, political party. But the South's one-party system was nothing like those that arose a little later in the twentieth century. It was nothing like the parties that emerged in Africa and Asia in the middle of the century, where the single party that had been the political instrument for achieving national independence from European colonial rule took over the reins of power and ruled many of these newly liberated nations for a number of decades without having to face an organized opposition party. Nor was the South's Democratic Party similar to the almost unchallenged Liberal Democratic Party that dominated Japan's politics for a half century since 1955 after its defeat in the Second World War. The Liberal Democrats' dominance ended in 2009, when they lost control to the Democratic Party of Japan (DPJ). It was also quite unlike the Institutional Revolutionary Party, the PRI, which had controlled Mexico from its revolution in 1911 until 2000, when the National Action Party (PAN) won the presidency. The PAN won again in 2006, only to fade and lose in 2008.

But there were obvious reasons for this sharp contrast with other one-party systems such as these. First, the southern Democrats were just an organized and self-conscious group within the ascendant national political party, and they actually governed only a segment of the national polity, namely, a dozen or so subunits of the governmental structure called states. And the particular states involved in this new party system were located in only one region of the country. This one-party system never possessed the nationwide political power of other prominent monopoly parties. Second, the South's dominant party was not a free-standing political organization, but a regional segment of one of the two national parties. And third, that national party was itself not a powerful, disciplined, monopolistic institution, since American political parties have been characteristically weak organizations by comparison with their equivalents elsewhere, in more centralized and unitary nation-states as well as in polities with parliamentary systems.

The South's one-party system was therefore quite unlike the one-party polities, or systems, that arose elsewhere in the twentieth century. In this international context, the southern system was certainly distinctive, even anomalous. But, if the South's twentieth-century one-party system was odd internationally, it was also unusual nationally. Nowhere else in the United States during the twentieth century was there anything remotely similar to the legal and institutionalized one-party system of the Solid South. Also out of step within the United States was the South's nineteenth-century experience of one-party dominance and hegemony. In no other region of the country was party politics so uncompetitive and for such a long period of time—almost the entire nineteenth century. Therefore, in each century, in the international as well as the national context, the one-party South was, to coin a phrase, "a peculiar political institution."

2

The Frontier and Filibuster Defense

ORIGINS AND DEVELOPMENT

For almost all of its history as part of the United States, the South has been on the defensive, fending off threats and attacks from outside its borders. The target of these aspersions and assaults was not the region's economy on the grounds that it presented a danger to the rest of the country or perhaps challenged powerful economic interests outside the South. Nor was the cause of offense the southern people's religious beliefs and customs or their cultural values and priorities. Instead, what really upset nonsoutherners was the South's system of race relations. No other feature of southern life provoked such displeasure as the region's manner of organizing its racial order—slavery for most of the nineteenth century and then segregation for most of the twentieth.

During these two eras of slavery and of segregation, the South was a minority within the nation. The region's population and the number of states it contained were both only slightly in the minority at the beginning of the dispute over slavery in the 1820s. But the South's proportion diminished steadily as population in the rest of the country grew rapidly through natural increase and immigration, and at the same time the number of states in the non-South increased. By the twentieth century, the South was a decided minority in a much-enlarged nation when the system of social segregation, and its political adjunct, disfranchisement, was challenged in the 1940s and after.

For a minority that is threatened, one of the most obvious strategies is to make a serious and judicious attempt to generate sympathy and support from elements within the majority. There are a number of ways of doing this. First, allies can be cultivated who either sympathize with the minority or can be encouraged to cooperate with it in exchange for some kind of *quid pro quo*. A second tactic is to defuse opposition by demonstrating a willingness to negotiate, yielding on matters that can be conceded without harming the minority's fundamental interests or practices. Concession of peripheral, nonessential matters might even strengthen the minority's position because it would demonstrate a willingness to engage in reasonable discussion and not try to force those who disagreed with it either to comply or else to capitulate. A third possible approach is to keep a low profile, recognizing that a strident stance will only draw attention to the problem in dispute and alienate likely sympathizers.

The advisability of discretion on the part of the minority South seemed obvious to Kenneth Rayner, a prominent Whig and slaveholder from North Carolina. He regretted by the 1850s that, in the South, "The Democratic party seems determined for political purposes, to keep up an endless agitation, on the subject of slavery. Just as one difficulty is settled, they reopen the agitation in some other shape." This approach was not only politically unwise, but it seemed counterproductive. For, in Rayner's view, "The true interest of a slave-holding community is a defensive one. The moral sense of the Christian world and of a large portion of our country is against us, in regard to slavery. We can't afford to be aggressive. We are in a minority."[1] Yet the South invariably took the aggressive route. This kind of response and the course of action that followed soon became generic and, as such, constituted one of the key elements of the southern political tradition.

THE AGGRESSIVE DEFENSE OF SLAVERY, 1830S

The political dispute over the admission of Missouri Territory to statehood in 1819 woke up Thomas Jefferson and the nation like "a fire bell in the night." The former president was correct in identifying this episode as a crisis. But whether the Missouri episode deserved to be considered a major threat to the South is far from clear. The placing of restrictions on the admission of Missouri Territory was certainly unprecedented because Missouri was on the verge of becoming a state in 1819. These requirements were imposed, therefore, not on a territory when it was being formed, but on a territory in its final stage just before it was admitted into the Union as a sovereign state.

Prior to 1819, slavery had encountered almost no opposition. It had expanded without hindrance into territories carved out of the Louisiana Purchase. It still existed in Illinois and Indiana, even though unofficially. It flourished under federal protection in the District of Columbia, the nation's capital. And finally, the United States government treated slavery as an integral part of the nation's social and economic order in its relations with foreign countries.[2] So slavery was an expanding and acknowledged feature of American life in 1819. Also reassuring to southern slave owners, Missouri itself was located on the northwestern fringe of those areas where the institution was established—in other words, far from the heartland of slavery. Even the provocative amendment to the Missouri statehood bill, proposed by James Tallmadge of New York, that precipitated the crisis did not touch slavery itself. It merely placed a limit on its increase by banning further slaves from entering Missouri and by freeing, at the age of twenty-five, all slave children born after statehood. The 10,000 slaves already in Missouri would remain in bondage until their death many decades later. Only their children would be freed, and even then only when they were adults in their mid-twenties. So slavery in Missouri was guaranteed another thirty to fifty years of existence.

The reaction among southern congressmen to the very prospect of gradual abolition was nevertheless massive and utterly uncompromising. Only three votes in both houses, all from border states, were cast by the slaveholding states in favor of the two parts of the Tallmadge amendment in February 1819. When the provisions were again voted on in 1820 as part of a group of measures that were called the Missouri Compromise, the South from the Gulf of Mexico to the Ohio River rejected them once again, but even more decisively this time—98–0. Even though the southerners had to concede the area north of the 36° 30' line to the free states and agree to the pairing of Missouri's admission with Maine's statehood, which were the terms of the compromise, the prize of keeping slavery pure and untrammeled was considered vital. Southern senators voted 20–2 for the entire compromise, which was what the southerners wanted, while northerners voted 18–4 against.[3]

The message of the Missouri crisis was clear. Even though it might take several generations to accomplish and might occur in a locality at the farthest point of the system's likely reach, any attempt to end slavery would be countered massively. At the same time, the lesson of the Tallmadge restrictions for the South was chilling. No one was questioning the jurisdiction of Congress over the territories and therefore its responsibility for protecting slavery in these embryonic states. But Tallmadge had conceived of the idea of imposing restrictions on slavery later in the process, at statehood in fact. And there was no constitutional provision that could be called upon to stop his amendment's extension of Congress's powers over the formation of territories to include the later admission of states—and maybe even into already established states like Missouri where slavery had existed for decades. Congressional guarantees and protections for slavery were therefore not worth the paper they were written on because justifications and interpretations could always be devised by men with interested motives for curbing and undermining the South's racial system. Moreover, any hostile action toward slavery put at risk the pecuniary value of existing slave property, even if slavery's actual existence was not directly threatened. In addition, there were numerous clauses in the Constitution, described pejoratively as the "elastic clauses," such as the general welfare clause, the guarantee of republican government clause, and the necessary and proper clause, that could be invoked in order to mobilize and expand federal power.

Over the decade and a half after the Missouri crisis, southern political leaders embarked on a campaign to shore up their defense of slavery with more substantive and material bulwarks than unreliable constitutional guarantees or good-faith understandings between political actors on the national stage. The initiative began when John Randolph of Roanoke made public on the floor of the House of Representatives the disquiet among Virginians like himself and Thomas Ritchie of the Richmond *Enquirer,* who called themselves "Old Republicans" and wanted to return to the strict constructionist principles of the original party of Jefferson. In a speech on the General Survey bill in January 1824, Randolph pointed out with alarm to "every man who has the misfortune to be and to have been born a slaveholder" that "if Congress possess the power to do what is proposed by this law [to promote federally financed internal improvements like roads and canals] . . . they may emancipate every slave in the United States, and with stronger color of reason than they can exercise the power now contended for."[4] The Constitution's "parchment barriers," a phrase coined by Madison, were simply no match for the many other clauses that allowed for the accretion of power and authority by the central government, or for the political power that could be wielded by a determined anti-slavery interest in Congress.

Randolph's lament that southern slavery lay exposed to the hostile winds of federal power was soon followed by the election of John Quincy Adams to the presidency later that same year. Adams was an avowed advocate of the American system, also espoused by his heir-apparent, Henry Clay, who was appointed secretary of state as a result of the "corrupt bargain" that supposedly secured Adams the presidency. At this pivotal moment, Martin Van Buren moved quickly to strengthen the forces of Andrew Jackson, the candidate who had just been denied the presidency by the Adams-Clay bargain, in preparation for the next presidential contest in 1828. Van Buren's plan aimed to revive the old Republican Party of Jefferson and thereby create a national party able to offset the dangers of sectional polarization and simultaneously thwart Adams's nationalist program. Since the South was to play a vital part in this reconfiguration of the Jacksonian coalition, John C. Calhoun and Thomas Ritchie were called on to play major roles. Calhoun was of critical importance. Previously an advocate of internal improvements "to bind the Republic together" and "conquer space" when he was a secretary of war in the late 1810s, he was now in an awkward position as vice-president in the Adams administration.[5] Calhoun's dilemma had arisen because he had undergone the equivalent of a conversion experience in the winter of 1825–26 when he realized, just like John Randolph, the danger to the South of increasing federal initiatives such as the ones President Adams was already pursuing with great zeal and energy. Soon, Calhoun would be attacking the protective tariff of 1828, "the Tariff of Abominations" as it was called, and employing his newly fashioned political weapon of nullification to prevent the tariff from being enforced in his own state of South Carolina.

Over the ensuing decade, the Democratic Party, with Jackson now in the presidency from 1828 until 1836 and its southern wing led by Calhoun, assaulted and eventually killed the American system. First, the protective tariff. Then, the national bank, the Second Bank of the United States. And finally, federal sponsorship of internal improvements in the form of a national infrastructure of roads, canals, and even railroads. Reflecting later on this episode, John Quincy Adams recalled to a friend in 1837:

> When I came to the presidency, the principle of internal improvement was swelling the tide of public prosperity, till the Sable Genius of the South [an unmistakable reference to Calhoun and the section he represented] saw the signs of his own inevitable downfall in the unparalleled progress of the general welfare of the North, and fell to cursing the tariff, and internal improvements, and raised the standard of free trade, nul-

> lification and state rights. I fell and with me fell, I fear never to rise again, certainly never to rise again in my day, the system of internal improvement by means of national energies.

After crediting the "Sable Genius of the South" with destroying his plans for the nation's economic development, the former president added wistfully, "The great object of my life . . . has failed."[6]

By portraying Calhoun as "the Sable Genius of the South" and making him the personification of the region he represented, Adams was assigning the blame for destroying his, Clay's, and the National Republican Party's vision of centrally directed and publicly promoted economic progress for the new and underdeveloped nation-state. And Calhoun was happy to take credit for this achievement. He told Daniel Webster in a debate on the Subtreasury bill in March 1838 that the New England senator was "right in fixing on 1825 as the year when my views in relation to the principles and character of the Government became firmly fixed and settled." In 1825, Calhoun recalled, he had examined carefully "the character and tendency of what was called, at the time, the American system, and saw clearly its oppressive, corrupting, and dangerous tendency. I took a firm stand against it."[7]

The result, he had announced in September 1837, was that "the days of legislative and executive encroachments, of tariffs and surpluses, of bank and public debt, and extravagant expenditure are past for the present. The Government stands in a position disentangled from the past, and freer to choose its future course than it ever has been since its commencement. We are about to take a fresh start. I move off under the State rights banner, and go in the direction in which I have been so long moving."[8]

This "fresh start" was not exclusively economic, however, for it also granted vital relief to the slaveholding South from the threat of an expanding central government, which, armed with the authority to build roads, could also use that authorization to free slaves. By restricting federal power by means of their judicial philosophy of state rights constitutionalism, the southern Democrats had succeeded in erecting a barrier to protect their region from the external menace that lay, no longer outside the country itself among hostile nations, but within it, in the nation's central government. To this end, the South's political leaders had, therefore, made two decisive moves by the mid-1830s. First, they had taken an unyielding stand against gradual abolition in states such as Missouri that were located on the geographic periphery of the slave system. Then, they had built another defensive barrier around slavery by disarming the federal government of its power to strike at slavery through its use of a contested authority to provide aid to economic development and to create a national bank and a protective tariff.

Even while these curbs on federal economic activism were actually under construction, the ultimate and much-feared threat to the system of slavery reared its head. This was the campaign to abolish slavery that arose in the northern states in the early 1830s. Very soon, its organizers had adopted the shrewd tactic of presenting petitions to Congress urging the abolition of slavery in the District of Columbia. The District was under the direct control of Congress; there, Congress exercised "exclusive jurisdiction in all cases whatsoever," according to Article 1, section 8, of the U.S. Constitution. The abolitionists believed that a victory over slavery was attainable there, since Congress was directly involved and the District was a small and quite marginal location in the world of slavery. Simultaneously, the petitioning process itself was a worthwhile tactic because it would mobilize support for abolition and publicize abolitionist activity at the national level. To the abolitionists' surprise perhaps, southern politicians saw this kind of activity as nothing short of menacing. In the winter of 1835–36, two of them, both from South Carolina and almost certainly acting in concert, challenged the entire operation. A newly elected congressman, James H. Hammond, and a political veteran, Senator John C. Calhoun, barred the door to the reception of abolition petitions and precipitated a confrontation that proved to be a defining moment in the simmering sectional conflict.

Prior to the two South Carolinians' initiative, petitions for the abolition of slavery in the District had been received and then passed on to the relevant committees. Either they went to the southern-dominated committees on the District in each house, where they were buried, or to a select committee appointed specially for the purpose of receiving them and then doing nothing about them. This was not good enough for Hammond and Calhoun. In his maiden speech, the younger Carolinian insisted that the House "put a more decided seal of reprobation on [petitions], by peremptorily rejecting them."[9] A month later, Calhoun demanded that the Senate not even receive them, but reject them outright. "We of the South are bound to resist it," Calhoun announced. "We will meet this question as firmly as if it were the direct question of emancipation in the States."[10] The ante could not have been upped any higher if simply receiving a petition about slavery in the federal district was considered tantamount to demanding abolition in South Carolina or Georgia.

To receive the petitions but not do anything about them, and certainly not even to discuss them, was a radical position. But to refuse even to receive them pushed the issue to its outer limits. But that was exactly where Calhoun wanted to take his stand. By refusing to receive the petitions, Congress would actually be refusing to recognize the petitioners—an important case to make because it denied formal recognition of the abolitionists, whom Calhoun considered "fanatics" and whose petitions were "a foul slander on nearly one-half of the States."[11] They should therefore be dismissed with contempt. To Calhoun's vivid imagination, the introduction of the petitions into Congress presented an even grimmer picture. Once the petitions came through the doors of Congress, Calhoun envisioned the question of abolition entering along with them. As a result, "we of the South" would be forced "to sit here, year after year, session after session, hearing ourselves and our constituents vilified by thousands [of petitions] . . . against which we must rise like culprits to defend ourselves, or permit them to go uncontradicted and unrestricted.

We must ultimately be not only degraded in our own estimation and that of the world, but be exhausted and worn out in such a contest."[12]

In the view of the late Don Fehrenbacher, this image of a defenseless South subjected to unceasing humiliation and degradation on the floor of Congress was precisely "the real issue that would drive the nation to civil war." And that issue was not slavery in the territories or the return of fugitive slaves, but "northern denunciation of slavery and whether it could be silenced."[13] *Speaking* against slavery in the halls of Congress, not even *acting* against it, was unacceptable and had therefore to be stopped in its tracks.

Calhoun's insistence that abolition petitions be rejected outright was based on his assumption that silencing talk about abolition was essential. In his main speech against receiving petitions on 9 March 1836, the South Carolinian explained, with the help of some graphic analogies, why the line had to be drawn here. The abolitionists were not waging a war of arms against southern slavery, he asserted. Instead, "The object is to humble and debase us . . . to blast our reputation, while they overthrow our domestic institutions." There was "but one way" to repel them, Calhoun declared. "We must meet the enemy on the frontier, on the question of receiving [petitions]; we must secure that important pass—it is our Thermopylae. The power of resistance, by universal law of nature, is on the exterior. Break through the shell, penetrate the crust, and there is no resistance within. . . . It is the first, the exterior question, that covers and protects all others," including ultimately the citadel, "slavery in the States."[14]

The language was, of course, Calhoun's alone: Identifying the frontier, taking a firm stand there, and not yielding an inch at this exterior line because penetration of the crust would result inexorably and inevitably in total defeat. But the attitude of mind it revealed shaped the "siege mentality" that gripped the region over the succeeding two decades. On a series of slavery-related issues, southerners staked out frontiers, exterior lines, upon which they took unyielding stands. Once these were conceded, it was believed, all would be lost. This was not a "last ditch" stand, but its very opposite—unyielding resistance at the "first ditch."

The outcome of the "great petition fight" of 1836 was a defeat for Calhoun and Hammond and their extreme position of outright rejection. Instead, a proposal from another South Carolinian, Representative Henry Laurens Pinckney, was adopted, requiring that petitions be received and then tabled automatically, without taking any action on them whatsoever. Practically, however, this achieved what Calhoun wanted, even though the petitions were not rejected altogether. The "gag rule," as Pinckney's procedure soon became known, obtained majorities in both houses of Congress. Despite ongoing attempts to remove it (and even a tightening of it in 1840), it was sustained until 1844 when the rule was finally repealed, thereby ungagging Congress. The contents of the petitions were not discussed in Congress for eight years. In practical terms, this was what Calhoun had wanted to achieve by his more extreme stand of unequivocal rejection.

Nevertheless, the tabling, and therefore the muzzling, of the petitions handed the abolitionists something of a victory. By attempting to frustrate, even deny, the right of petition as well as to suppress talk and free speech about slavery, the southerners provided the abolitionists with another, and perhaps unanticipated, issue—the infringement of civil liberties. This broadened their appeal and support beyond the initial question of abolition in the District of Columbia. A southern senator, John P. King of Georgia, had warned Calhoun of this likelihood in one of the first debates on petitions in February 1836. Confronting Calhoun on the Senate floor, he had warned: "Sir, if southern Senators were actually in the pay of the directory of Nassau Street [a reference to the New York headquarters of the Tappan brothers, who were wealthy merchants and leading abolitionists], they could not more effectively cooperate in the views and administer to the wishes of these enemies to the peace and quiet of our country."[15] As the gag rule continued to be denounced in Congress and in the newspapers during its eight-year existence, the civil liberties issue further increased the abolitionists' acceptability in the North as defenders of the First Amendment's protection of free speech and the right of petition, while it also maintained public awareness of abolition as an ongoing matter of national concern. By taking such an advanced position and foreclosing discussion, the southerners were allowing their "fanatical" adversaries to appear the reasonable and wronged party.

THE AGGRESSIVE DEFENSE OF SEGREGATION, 1920S AND 1930S

Let us now move on almost a century later, to the 1920s, when the South's post-slavery system of race relations had assumed legal and official form and had been in operation for just over two decades. In 1921, a bill was introduced into the House to make lynching a federal crime. This was the very first occasion on which the national government took any formal action to challenge the Jim Crow system of legal segregation and disfranchisement that had been imposed on the region around the turn of the century at the insistence of the South's dominant Democratic Party. After Woodrow Wilson became president in 1913, the federal government introduced segregation into many of its own departments and facilities and even oversaw the segregation of public transportation in the nation's capital. To the white South's great satisfaction, its new system of racial segregation was thereby given official recognition and legitimacy.

The anti-lynching bill was sponsored by Leonidas Dyer, a Republican from St. Louis. Declaring lynching a felony, the bill defined a lynch mob as "five or more persons acting in concert" and outside the legal process, in order to kill someone as punishment for committing "an actual or supposed public offense." If found guilty, the lynchers would be imprisoned for a minimum of five years, while the county where the lynching occurred would be fined $10,000 to pay compensation to the family of the victim.[16] This measure resulted from pressure exerted on the Republican Party by the NAACP to take some action against the outbreak of lynchings that had been going on ever since the 1880s and had claimed close to four thousand lives, a horrendous figure of roughly one hundred each year. After declining to below one hundred in the early twentieth century, that number had suddenly peaked again in 1917–19 at the end of the First World War. Initially a predominantly southern phenomenon, lynching was now occurring throughout the country. And so the Republicans pledged in their 1920 platform to "consider" federal legislation. When the election elevated Warren G. Harding to the presidency and gave the party a massive majority of almost two hundred in the House, the Republicans decided to take legislative action.

Southern members of the House Judiciary Committee raised only a few objections when hearings were held on the bill in 1921. Mostly, they claimed it was a cynical ploy aimed at winning black votes in northern cities such as Dyer's own St. Louis. They asserted contemptuously that the bill was evidence of the Republican Party's feebleness in the face of pressure from the recently formed African American protest organization, the NAACP. But when the Dyer bill reached the House floor, southern Democrats unleashed a torrent of invective against the measure. A compendium of the charges against the bill was laid out by William W. Larson of Georgia, who denounced it as "an Act to assassinate State rights; to nullify the constitutions of the several States; to corrupt public morals; to encourage rape and race riots; and to pension the families of rapists and despoilers of society."[17] During the five or six days when the bill was debated, southern Democrats held the floor most of the time, while its Republican supporters interjected on occasion merely to ask questions and remonstrate against the southern onslaught.

As Larson's list revealed, the primary charge against the measure was its subversion of the American governmental system by destroying the sovereignty and independence of the states. Hatton W. Sumners of Texas, the ranking Democrat on the Judiciary Committee, explained that the anti-lynching bill would "complete the reduction of the States to a condition of vassalage." By taking over the states' police power, the measure was "dynamiting the governmental structure," he concluded.[18]

Speaker after speaker opened his remarks by protesting that the bill was unconstitutional and would result in state legislatures having, as Fred H. Dominick of South Carolina predicted, "no more powers than township commissioners."[19] Another South Carolinian, James Byrnes, who would later become Harry Truman's secretary of state, imagined "an army of Federal police, who must invade the state to secure evidence." His imagination running wild, Byrnes even suggested that, whereas lynch mobs "violate the law," congressmen who proposed the Dyer bill to punish lynchers were "willing to violate the Constitution." They were more culpable than the lynchers, whose "act is in heat and passion, [while] yours [is] in calm deliberation."[20]

The dire danger facing the South from Dyer's proposal to make lynching a federal crime was stressed constantly and in words as menacing and frenzied as those uttered by Byrnes. "Not since the formation of the Federal government has a more important legislative proposition addressed itself to the consideration of the Congress," intoned Congressman Sumners.[21] "If this bill can be enacted into law then the entire fabric of our Government is torn to shreds" was the ominous warning from Congressman Patrick H. Drewry of Louisiana.[22] From time to time, Calhoun's admonition to draw the line at the frontier, or all was lost, appeared during the debate. On the opening day, Finis J. Garrett of Tennessee urged resistance to the Dyer bill because it would "cut the anchor and set the constitution adrift . . . it will not stop with the exigency that causes the act [that is, punishing lynchers] but it will float on and on, a wreck upon an uncharted ocean" until "the whole fine fabric of this Republic [will] be gone forever."[23] The language of John J. McSwain of South Carolina even resembled Calhoun's when he called "the effort to pass this anti-lynching bill . . . an assault upon the last defensive ditch around the citadel of State's rights."[24] The anti-lynching bill had to be resisted, or else the states would become vassals of the national government and their sovereign rights be destroyed. In effect, the bill represented the frontier, at which the enemy had to be confronted and beaten back.

But why was this particular bill that was intended to punish, and even prevent, the hideous practice of lynching and to protect its potential victims, deemed the Thermopylae of state rights? Why did southern Democrats feel compelled to take their stand on a measure so eminently reasonable and humane? Would they not lose respect and credibility by denouncing an attempt to curb so horrible a crime as the hanging, or burning to death, of a victim who was not only denied a trial but might well be completely innocent? A Missouri congressman, Edgar C. Ellis, expressed concern that the Dyer bill had had "the effect of a depth bomb dropped in our midst. The deeps of partisan and sectional feeling have been thrown into violent commotion." Yet, Congressman Ellis continued, all of this fury and antagonism had been stirred up by a proposal that simply provided for the national government to assert its "inherent right and power to protect its citizens from mobs and to preserve its very life and conserve its civilization."[25] Instead of acknowledging the barbarity and lawlessness of lynching, the South's congressmen rose up in solid phalanx to excuse it. Frequently, they even justified lynching as a white man's instinctive and unquenchable lust for retribution against a rapist, presumed to be black, who had, it was claimed, violated a white woman.

Ellis regretted that, in defending their position, the southerners trotted out "the old, pestiferous bugaboo of State rights." This familiar, knee-jerk reaction was accompanied, the Missourian continued, by an argument that "would make lynching an essential and [they] would have us believe that by the people of the South it is thought to be an essential."[26] Ellis was in fact convinced that the leaders of southern opinion—its newspapers, religious leaders, educators—did not see the issue the way the congressional delegation did. Yet the region's congressmen made it appear that the South was solidly behind them. Moreover, Ellis continued, lynching was not an essential feature of the South's system of race relations and therefore staking so much on its defense was politically unwise. A similar observation was made the following year when the bill was debated in the Senate. Walter E. Edge of New Jersey was pretty sure that no senator, not even a southern one, "would permit lynching over proper court trials." So, he wondered, "why can it be any reflection upon a State if the Government . . . offers it cooperation and assistance [so] that a fair trial will be given any man accused of crime—murder or whatever the offence may be?"[27]

At first glance, it does seem puzzling that the southern delegation chose to dig in its heels on the very first occasion since the establishment of the Jim Crow system when federal legislation relating to race was introduced. Why not collaborate on a measure favoring orderly trials over lynch law, especially when lynching was not by any means confined to the South? That way, the South could not so easily be denounced as a haven for lynch mobs. Nor would a defense of segregation be identified with a defense of lynching. To defend lynching as an essential part of the southern race relations system was, as Ellis had indicated in the House, a sure way to give the system a bad name. Far better to wait and take a stand on an issue, should one arise, that was not only more crucial but easier to justify and defend. Instead, the frontier and Thermopylae analogies were invoked once again as the South allowed itself to become identified with lawlessness and atrocities, just as a century earlier it had become the enemy of free speech and the right of petition by keeping abolition petitions out of Congress.

This "all or nothing," "line in the sand" mentality, and the paranoia that accompanied it, were all too evident whenever southern congressmen discussed the matter that was really at issue, namely, their social system of white supremacy. To defend it, they deployed state rights and whatever rhetorical weapons they could lay their hands on. That the racial system was the citadel they were defending was evident as the debate continued over the Dyer bill. After denouncing the bill because it was unconstitutional and destructive of state sovereignty, every speaker expounded on the difficult race problem facing the South and how southern whites were grappling with it responsibly and successfully. "The eternal race question," as John Rankin of Mississippi termed it, was a problem that, in the opinion of Louisiana's John N. Sandlin, was "the most momentous which has confronted any people in any age."[28]

By keeping the races separate, white southerners believed they had produced what Hatton Sumners felt was "a fairly workable arrangement."[29] But it was precarious and easily upset by meddling outsiders who thought they understood the situation, and African Americans in general, much better. In an observation worthy of Donald Rumsfeld, George Bush's often befuddled secretary of defense, Sumners warned: "I know that you know that you do not know much about this question. You had better let us alone who live there We have a pretty hard time of it now." But he quickly shifted the onus onto northerners, who would soon have a race problem of their own, since African Americans were migrating in large numbers to northern cities. "They are drifting in your direction," he observed gleefully, "and you are going to understand this question better some day."[30] Indeed, Sumners and most of the southern speakers were delighted to be able to point to the racial friction and problems already breaking out in the North, in the form of the ugly postwar incidents in Chicago, East St. Louis, and Tulsa, where rioting whites had attacked blacks, resulting in the loss of many lives and considerable destruction of property.

Even though lynching was not an essential part of the South's racial system, southern Democrats feared any intervention from outside because it might upset their control over a situation they considered not entirely secure. Moreover, interference implied that they did not know how to run their own affairs. Over and over again, the southerners insisted that, as Representative James P. Woods of Virginia saw it, they were discharging their "responsibility . . . in good faith," and "the southern white man is to-day the Negro's best friend." Any attempt to interfere in a matter "peculiarly theirs, will be met with disfavor, if not, indeed, with resentment on the part of the South."[31]

This feeling of resentment was often cited in the southerners' speeches. Hallett S. Ward of North Carolina used the word several times in his speech, explaining that the Dyer bill was "insulting" to the southern states and would provoke "their righteous resentment."[32] Whereas the debates over abolition petitions were likely, in Calhoun's view, to produce feelings of "degradation" among the southern congressmen who had to listen to criticisms of their racial practices, the anti-lynching bill provoked "resentment" that southerners' best efforts at solving their own race problem were being questioned.

This attitude of "resentment" was evident from the moment the Dyer bill reached the Senate in November 1922, many months after passing the House on a convincing vote of 231 to 119, with 74 not voting. Deriding the measure as a "force bill," Alabama's Oscar W. Underwood, the Democratic leader in the Senate, announced defiantly: "It is not going to become a law at this session of Congress."[33] The region's senators were, he already knew, a unit in opposition. As he readily revealed, "I have not conferred with them as in a conference, that was not necessary." For every southern Democrat knew full well that the measure was to be resisted and a filibuster was being organized to prevent its passage. "Pass it if you can," Underwood threatened the Republicans; "abandon it if we force you to do so."[4] And he continued: "This proposition is fundamental. We regard this bill as a rape of the Constitution. We regard this bill as an infringement of the liberties of our people and the freedom of our State governments, and we feel that we are justified in making any attack on it."[34]

After five days of delay and obstruction, Henry Cabot Lodge announced that the Republican majority "would not press the bill further," since it could not produce enough votes to end the filibuster that was tying up Senate business and was likely to continue to do so for several more months.[35] Now the majority leader in the Senate, Lodge when a freshman congressman in 1890–91 had been closely identified with the last "force bill," the federal elections bill known more generally as the Lodge bill. This bill had also gone down to defeat at the hands of a Senate filibuster, effectively ending the federal government's attempt to supervise elections in the South after Reconstruction and at the same time protect the right to vote guaranteed by the Fifteenth Amendment.

On the first attempt to pass national legislation that in any way affected the South's system of racial segregation in the twentieth century, the region's congressmen rose up in righteous indignation, in "resentment" that their rights and their good-faith attempts to deal with "the eternal race question" were being challenged and impugned. They pledged themselves to go to *any* lengths to prevent *any* interference by the federal government, even an effort to curb an ugly excess like lynching. As before, this stance required resistance at the first ditch, at the "frontier," at the "exterior line." And, once again, Oscar Underwood explained perfectly what was at stake. "The only way we can fight it," he explained, "and make the majority understand we are fighting it and let the country understand we will always fight such a measure [that is, any 'force bill'] is to simply obstruct legislation until we come to an understanding about it."[36] By "understanding" he meant, not an amended bill produced as a result of negotiation, but a decision by the majority to withdraw the bill altogether, after failing to shut off debate and defeat the threatened filibuster.

In the late 1930s, several serious attempts were again made to enact federal anti-lynching legislation. The two major efforts were mounted by Robert Wagner of New York, a leading Democrat who sponsored the critical labor relations and housing laws of the Second New Deal. Because anti-lynching bills were assured of passage in the House, the first renewed attempt focused on the Senate, where the filibuster was a procedural weapon always available to the southerners. In April 1935, just three days of debate on the Costigan-Wagner bill was all that was needed to reveal that the supermajority of votes to obtain cloture was simply unattainable.[37] The mere threat of a filibuster, as in 1922, proved enough to get the bill withdrawn.

Three years later, another anti-lynching measure, the Wagner–Van Nuys bill, was introduced into the Senate. This time, the filibuster was actually needed. It lasted from 6 January to 21 February 1938, after two cloture votes had been taken and failed and after Allen Ellender of Louisiana had held the floor for 27 hours and 45 minutes over the course of six days. With the southerners able and willing to talk the bill to death, and with no way to close off debate because its supporters lacked the sixty-seven votes to shut off debate, its sponsors gave up and withdrew the measure. Yet again, the "understanding" required earlier by Oscar Underwood had been obtained, for the South's enemy had capitulated, as before.[38]

Calhoun's frontier analogy, and the mind-set that gave rise to it, were clearly on display during the six-week-long filibuster against the Wagner–Van Nuys bill. No senator exhibited this southern state of mind more convincingly than the forty-year-old Georgian Richard B. Russell, who would become the undisputed head of the Southern Caucus for two decades, from 1946 to 1968. In a speech that dragged on for several days in late January 1938, he denounced the "unnecessary and uncalled-for anti-lynching bill." Russell believed it was intended simply as a test of southern resolve, "the opening wedge . . . for other legislation of this type that we know will certainly follow." Yielding on this seemingly innocuous measure was fatal, Russell feared, because it actually represented "the first step in a program of such far-reaching importance and of such dire effect and consequences that it would strike down the civilization of the States which sent us to this body." The "program" that Russell was convinced would follow consisted of measures "to control the requirements of suffrage and the qualifications of voters" within the states; "to enforce social equality . . . wiping out all segregation of the races"; and "to strike down the laws of the several States which prevent the intermarriage of whites and blacks."[39]

Defeat on the anti-lynching issue would clear the path for this program aimed at dismantling the South's racial order. Therefore, successful resistance at the frontier was vital to prevent the federal government from entering the South's racial domain. Just as Calhoun had insisted that the abolitionists and their program were to be kept out of Congress, now Richard Russell was demanding that the liberal, northern Democrats were to be kept out of the South.

3

The Frontier and Filibuster Defense

FINAL PHASE

During the decade of the 1940s, another facet of the South's racial system became a target for northern Democrats. This time, it was the poll tax. Every southern state had made payment of this head tax a prerequisite for voting when they had revised their constitutions during the disfranchisement campaigns at the turn of the twentieth century. Although this fee for the privilege of voting had been very effective as a disfranchising device, it was by no means the only obstacle that many voters, especially African Americans, encountered when they tried to register or cast their ballots. Literacy and residential tests, the white primary, and intimidation and obstruction by hostile registration and election officials also prevented them from voting. Nevertheless, southern congressmen considered poll-tax repeal a serious threat. And on three occasions, in each of the Congresses during the 1940s, they mounted an offensive to obstruct repeal and eventually defeat it.

The first showdown over the poll tax occurred in 1941–42 after a discharge petition had managed to pry loose from the House Judiciary Committee, now chaired by Hatton Sumners, a repeal bill that the Texan had kept bottled up there for three years. In the House debate that ensued, Mississippi's William Colmer raised the alarm. "The direct object of this movement is to enfranchise the negro," he warned. "If Congress can remove the poll tax requirement it can also remove educational requirements and [even] registration itself."[1] Leading the attack in the Senate, Theodore Bilbo, also from Mississippi, dreaded the consequences of a successful assault on the poll tax, since it would "open the floodgates" and allow the power of the federal government to pour into the South and inundate its electoral system. "If the poll tax bill passes, the next step will be an effort to remove the registration qualification, the educational qualification of negroes. If that is done, we will have no way of preventing negroes from voting."[2]

Once again, southern congressmen decided to take their stand at the frontier. On the very first occasion that the region's system of disfranchisement was challenged in Congress, they resorted immediately to their traditional strategy by mobilizing to prevent any breach at the frontier, at their outer line of defense, that would lead inexorably, so they believed, to the undermining of the entire electoral structure. Yet the repeal bill was a federal measure dealing only with federal elections, so the intricate system of voter restrictions that shaped state and local elections within each state would remain secure and beyond the bill's purview. Moreover, three southern states—North Carolina (1920), Louisiana (1934), and Florida (1937)—had already repealed their state-imposed poll-tax requirement, with little harm done to the racial hierarchy. White registration had increased, just as the advocates of repeal had intended, while the registered black vote remained almost the same, thanks to the vigilance of hostile white registrars.

But the very idea of federal intrusion into the South's voting procedures had to be resisted decisively. In 1942, after endless diversionary tactics in the Senate and a filibuster lasting eight days, the vote to terminate debate failed to obtain the two-thirds of "those present and voting" required by the Senate's Rule 22. In fact, the advocates of repeal could not even generate a simple majority, let alone the required two-thirds, since the vote to close off debate, called cloture, was thirty-seven for and forty-one against. Two years later, when poll-tax repeal was again before the Senate, cloture was once more defeated by thirty-six to forty-four after just a couple of days of debate. In these votes, Republicans and northern Democrats, each numbering about a dozen, joined the twenty or so southerners in preventing cloture. But in 1946, when a poll-tax repeal bill was yet again presented to the Senate after another overwhelming endorsement in the House, the vote to end debate received, much to the southerners' surprise, a majority of the votes cast.[3] Even though the required two-thirds was still out of reach, it was close enough this time to warrant an assertive countermeasure, which arose in the form of an enhanced and toughened filibuster.

The filibuster, or just the mere threat of it, had become the essential weapon in the South's battle to protect its racial order. This device was relied on to prevent any breach in the wall that the region's political leaders had, in their own minds, built up around their system of racial subordination. Any measure that was threatening, or just looked likely to be so, had to be kept out. As Richard Russell, who replaced Tom Connally as the leader of the Southern Caucus around 1946, was fully aware, the Senate represented "the last weapon against the tyranny and statism and the mood of the mob." Without the filibuster and the two-thirds rule to sustain it, "it will be very simple for them to pass so-called civil rights measures."[4] South Carolina's Olin Johnston concurred that, "as long as we have [the] filibuster available as an effective weapon of defense and there are enough of us within the ranks," civil rights initiatives could assuredly be repelled.[5]

But, by 1946, the situation was looking dire as the vote in favor of cloture approached a majority. To guard against this danger, the rules governing the Senate's practice of "continuous debate" had to be strengthened. Russell proceeded to take care of this in early 1949. The growing peril facing the South was generated by developments outside the Senate, and even outside the United States. Racial and ethnic discrimination had been pervasive during the Second World War, and a powerful reaction against it became evident in Europe and the United States after the war was over. Moreover, thousands of black servicemen had returned to America expecting better treatment and less overt discrimination after their sacrifices in the war. Finally, the emerging Cold War contest with the Soviet Union put America on notice to address its system of racial discrimination, especially the legally sanctioned version of it in the South.

This shift in public perception provided both the stimulus and the context for the urban, liberal Democrats from the North, who had challenged southern racial practices in the 1930s, to engage in the struggle against discrimination with more vigor and conviction. No longer could southern Democrats dismiss this opposition as merely partisan and politically motivated. Instead, they began to recognize that the South confronted, not a limited political campaign, but a cause that was unlikely to go away or peter out. This fear became tangible in 1948 when Harry S. Truman, the Democratic president who had succeeded Franklin Roosevelt, unveiled a civil rights agenda and planned to run on it for reelection. Truman's initiative was approved, and even expanded, by the Democratic Party's national convention, when a civil rights plank was included in its election platform. In response, several southern delegations walked out in protest, while the remainder rallied behind the candidacy of Russell himself, who obtained 262 votes for the party's presidential nomination. Bitter in defeat, his supporters proceeded to defy party custom by refusing to make Truman's nomination unanimous.

When, to almost everyone's surprise, Truman emerged victorious from the election, Senate Democrats moved quickly to clip the southerners' wings with an attempt to expand Rule 22 so as to require procedural motions, not just legislative measures themselves, to be bound by the limitations of cloture. Richard Russell and the Southern Caucus saw this gambit as dangerous in itself, but also quite possibly a precedent for a further demand that debate be ended by a simple majority of the votes cast, not the prevailing two-thirds. This possibility, which would essentially terminate the protection provided by cloture's required supermajority, was what the southerners believed was their opponents' eventual goal.[6]

So they launched a filibuster against the rule change. It lasted several weeks and was eventually resolved by an arrangement that clearly benefited the South. Russell conceded that motions could be bound by cloture, but in exchange he obtained a change in the definition of two-thirds, increasing it from those "present and voting" to include the entire membership of the Senate, currently numbering sixty-four. Also removed from the restrictions of cloture was any discussion and debate over rules changes. As a result, a debate over changes in Senate rules could not be cut off, thus allowing for interminable filibusters and making it almost impossible to make any future change in the terms of debate. Faced by a challenge to the almighty filibuster, the southerners, ably led by Russell, had outmaneuvered their opponents and actually strengthened the procedural mechanism that was their preeminent and essential weapon.[7]

Soon after this victory, southern Democrats had to deal with another threat—the insistent demand for a Fair Employment Practices Committee that had arisen just before America's entry into World War II and would continue throughout the 1940s. The idea of an FEPC had emerged rather suddenly in 1941 when A. Philip Randolph, head of the Brotherhood of Sleeping-Car Porters and leader of the March on Washington Movement, raised the issue as the United States prepared to enter the war. Randolph had called for a rally in the nation's capital to demand that the federal government agree not to discriminate against African Americans when the anticipated wartime expansion of federal hiring commenced. Anxious to head off a public protest at such a critical moment, President Roosevelt issued Executive Order 8802, creating a committee to ensure that firms contracting with the military did not discriminate. But the FEPC was a weak instrument. Its duration was only temporary. It could issue no general directives, but simply receive complaints. And it did not even have the authority to enforce its own decisions. Nevertheless, the South was worried. So the chairman of the FEPC, who was actually a southerner—Mark Etheridge of the *Louisville Courier-Journal*—reassured the region that "Executive Order 8802 is a war order, and not a social document." Furthermore, "there is no power in the world . . . which could now force the Southern white people to the abandonment of the principle of social segregation."[8] Despite these reassuring signs, the South's senators continued to be seriously alarmed. As they saw it, the committee was a Trojan horse that had managed to get inside the region's defense perimeter, the point at which the anti-lynching and anti–poll-tax campaigns had been fought out successfully. The FEPC moved the threat past that perimeter, past the frontier, toward the citadel—the South's system of racial segregation.

Over the course of the decade, successful assaults on the FEPC were waged in the Senate, with southerners in the lead. In 1944, its small appropriation of $1 million was cut in half, while jurisdiction over the committee was moved from the executive branch to Congress, where southern congressmen could exercise oversight through the relevant committees they chaired and controlled. Since an outright assault involving the threat of a filibuster was deemed unwise and unpatriotic in time of war, the FEPC danger was defused, rather than destroyed by a pitched battle. But in 1946, with the war ended, the South's preferred mode of operation was employed when a bill was introduced into the Senate to make the FEPC permanent. This move had been anticipated, and Richard Russell, who had led the wartime campaign to weaken the FEPC, also took charge of the fight to eliminate it.

Because it was not considered an influential agency and its authority was quite limited, the FEPC has not been given as much attention by historians as the dramatic legislative battles over the more clearly defined issues of lynching and the poll tax. Yet the FEPC was perhaps considered more dangerous because it was insidious. After all, the committee was not aimed specifically at the South's racial system and it did not provoke public indignation or channel southern anger, as the other two issues did. But the South's national representatives imagined that the FEPC posed a fundamental threat to the region's structure of white domination and control. Unlike lynching and poll taxes, a federal agency that was charged with prohibiting racial discrimination by employers clearly interfered with the South's system of labor control, and necessarily with its racial system as well. Unless resisted, federal investigation of racial discrimination in the workplace would soon expand into other areas of southern life and endanger the system of segregation itself. Corrosive yet less visible, this threat had to be stopped dead in its tracks by eliminating the FEPC altogether.

In 1946, Richard Russell and the Southern Caucus mobilized the region's heavy artillery against the bill to make the FEPC permanent. Even though their intended filibuster of the vote to bring the bill to the floor was frustrated at the outset by a surprise procedural maneuver, the southerners threw everything into their obstructionist strategy in the debate on the measure itself. As an opener, they obstructed the business of the Senate by insisting that the official journal of the body's proceedings be read and altered. After four days of this annoying and provocative exercise had shown that the caucus meant business and was settling in for the long haul, the southerners switched to the pending measure itself. In his speech opening the debate, Harry F. Byrd of Virginia threatened that the South's senators would "stand together on the question as firmly as on any issue affecting our southern people which has ever been raised."[9] For an entire week, they spoke endlessly about the FEPC and its dangers. Eventually, a motion to end the filibuster was introduced, and as expected, it failed to obtain the required two-thirds majority. The permanent FEPC had been defeated.

But elimination of the FEPC threat did not give the southerners the feeling of security and closure that they had experienced after their successes against the anti-lynching and anti–poll-tax legislation. They had triumphed as before; yet the opposition had actually increased in size, while its composition had begun to change. The vote on cloture had revealed a majority in favor, consisting of 22 Democrats and 26 Republicans, but the South's support had declined to 36. This was the first time a majority had approved cloture on an issue deemed critical to southern Democrats. More alarming was the behavior of many of the Republicans. Evidently, they considered a permanent FEPC an acceptable idea. Indeed, the party of Lincoln seemed to be realizing that it needed to be more assertive if it was to retain its traditional support among African Americans in the North. Otherwise, they might lose them to the Democratic Party, whose increasingly liberal and urban base was aligning it with the interests of northern blacks.

Faced with the reality of a declining number of votes to sustain a filibuster and a broadening bipartisan attack on their region's racial order, the Southern Caucus, as the front line of the region's resistance, had to reassess its strategy. The emergence of Richard Russell of Georgia as the leader of the caucus in the late 1940s coincided with the changing circumstances that the South faced. And the suave, highly respected, but politically shrewd and powerful Russell was just the right senator to steer the caucus in a new direction. As North Carolina's Sam Ervin observed much later, "Dick Russell always carried on his combat in such a knightly fashion that he never aroused the antagonism of the people most determined to overcome his efforts. He had an easy capacity to do that."[10] Accordingly, the Southern Caucus began to organize its forces and plan its operations more carefully than previously under the direction of Tom Connally of Texas. The caucus needed also to supplement its core vote of 22 southerners with support from senators outside the region. And these allies had to be convinced that the southerners were more than mere obstructionists who lacked a cause that others could respect, or perhaps even agree with. So the aim was to use the debates as, in Russell's words, "an educational campaign" to inform senators of the content of each measure and make sure they understood how dangerous each of them was to the values and institutions of the country as a whole, not just the South.

Of course, the southern senators had previously denounced the antilynching and anti–poll-tax bills as unconstitutional and undesirable, but now the criticism was to be made in more measured tones and with the racial, and specifically southern, features of the region's case downplayed. And finally, as conclusive evidence that willful obstruction was not the criterion, the caucus had to demonstrate a willingness to negotiate over legislation, and even propose amendments. In other words, the strategy would be to change and improve measures deemed hostile, rather than reflexively denounce and defeat them. A modified, even weakened, bill might prove more palatable to the southerners, thereby obviating the need to defeat it in its unamended form. By participating in the give-and-take of the legislative process, the South might also demonstrate that its senators were active participants and responsible legislators, not merely angry outliers.

The need for this shift in strategy became even more evident in 1948, when President Truman announced his civil rights agenda as a key element in his reelection campaign. Endorsing most of the recommendations contained in *To Secure These Rights,* the report submitted by the civil rights commission he had appointed in 1946, Truman made clear his intention of winning the votes of African Americans in the North in the 1948 election and attaching them firmly to the Democratic Party. Truman proceeded on a broad front. Executive action alone was required to accomplish three of the report's recommendations—to end discrimination in the federal civil service, to integrate the armed forces, and to create a U.S. civil rights commission. But Congress was responsible for enacting other proposals—such as the bills to end the poll tax and make the FEPC permanent—that Truman and his party seemed determined to implement, despite their numerous past defeats on both issues. For the first time, the executive branch had taken the initiative on civil rights and antidiscrimination, and it had done so, not by espousing a single issue, but by gathering together a number of them into an agenda of changes considered necessary to end racial discrimination and achieve equal rights. To make matters worse, the Democratic Party seemed poised to commit itself to this broad agenda. Yet this was the very same party to which the southerners had irrevocably attached themselves and their region's security since Reconstruction.

Southern senators could therefore no longer operate as an isolated minority capable of defeating legislative assaults on the region's racial order, one bill at a time, until the attackers grew tired and gave up. Instead, they faced what appeared to be a campaign to change "the southern way of life," in which the executive branch and the Democratic Party had enlisted. The filibuster was still the southerners' indispensable weapon, but they needed more votes to sustain it and more allies to enable them to work the political machinery of the federal government, within which they already had considerable influence, especially in Congress's committee system. After successfully strengthening the cloture rule in spring 1949, Russell acknowledged privately that "this was only one battle in a war that will be waged increasingly against us."[11] And it was a war that could not be won. It could, however, be prolonged and the showdown delayed. As Keith M. Finley has demonstrated in his *Delaying the Dream,* this approach became the Southern Caucus's operating assumption by the late 1940s.[12]

After his surprise victory in 1948, Truman introduced both the poll-tax and permanent FEPC bills. Despite the momentum provided by the president's initiative and his vindication at the polls, both measures failed. In fact, the poll-tax repeal was defeated twice because Truman had brought it up before the election in a special session during July 1948. After passing the House by the largest majority thus far, the measure obtained the support of the Republican leadership in the Senate in the belief that it would encourage black northerners to vote Republican in the upcoming election. But once procedural objections began to be raised, the Republicans backed off. They again revealed that they had no stomach for a protracted debate in 1949 when Truman tried once more to get the poll tax repealed. Helping to defuse the initiative for repeal was a pledge by the Southern Caucus to end the tax by constitutional amendment, rather than by statute. This method was actually preferred by southern Democrats because it would involve state action only, through the constitutional requirement that states ratify any amendment. By contrast, a federal law might necessitate the intervention of the federal government to get the southern states to comply. But there the matter rested for another decade until the Kennedy administration revived the proposal in 1962. Two years later, the poll tax was ended when the Twenty-fourth Amendment was enacted and then ratified.

Equally decisive was the fate of the permanent FEPC that President Truman proposed after his election. Before the bill reached the Senate, the upper chamber had revised its cloture rule. Instead of loosening it, as most northern Democrats had hoped, the outcome was, as we saw earlier, an agreement that allowed cloture on motions but raised the number of votes required to achieve it. Armed with a strengthened filibuster, the southern Democrats were confident they could kill the FEPC yet again in 1950. They embarked upon the now-familiar "educational campaign" and a more national and judicious explanation of their objections to the measure; after nine days, the proponents of the FEPC called for a vote to end the filibuster (for that is what it was, despite the more elevated tone of the remarks). And cloture was defeated, 52–32, twelve votes short of the new requirement of 64. But there was now a strong majority in favor, because all but six of the 39 Republicans supported cloture, a sharp contrast with their weakness on poll-tax repeal. Had the cloture requirement not been tightened, the southern Democrats' margin of safety would have been close to breachable in 1949 and 1950.

The southerners' ability to repel civil rights legislation with their revised "frontier and filibuster defense" would not be tested again until the late 1950s. Before then, a Republican, Dwight D. Eisenhower, was in the White House and the Democrats' majority in the Senate had been whittled down to just one or two seats, even becoming a minority in the 83rd Congress, 1953–55. Meanwhile, the rise of anti-Communist hysteria provoked by Cold War fears and the Red Scare tactics of Joe McCarthy made the liberals hesitate to press for legislative remedies in their campaign against southern segregation, both inside Congress and out. Any course of action that could conceivably ignite anxiety about federal interference undermining state sovereignty and individual freedom was certain to be denounced as "un-American" and "Communistic."

While the executive and legislative branches were keeping a low profile, the judiciary, however, appeared undeterred. In 1954, the Supreme Court handed down its landmark decision, *Brown v. Board of Education,* which called for an end to legal segregation of the South's public schools. Despite the successful efforts of its senators to defend the region from hostile legislation at the frontier in Congress, the Supreme Court seemed to have allowed the federal government to enter into the very institutions of white control inside the region itself, into its public schools no less. Attention now focused on the effort to prevent the desegregation of southern schools. This time, the frontier, the line in the sand, was not located in the U.S. Senate, but at the local schoolhouse door.

In the South's response to *Brown,* the lead would be taken, not by U.S. senators, but by state governors. Initially, a measured response called "local option" seemed to be the course to pursue. A complicated procedure of gradual and limited compliance, local option devolved onto school boards the responsibility for devising and implementing plans for token desegregation of a district's schools. The state's role would be to pass pupil assignment laws permitting students to be moved to schools on a nonracial basis, such as academic performance or suitability to attend a particular school. But most governors were reluctant to follow this path and soon swung into line behind the strategy of "massive resistance" being promoted by Harry Byrd and his statewide political machine in Virginia. This course of action was tantamount to noncompliance or, in the terminology used by Byrd, "interposition," which was another word for Calhoun's doctrine of nullification. In practical terms, a state would take over the public schools and close them if it chose to do so, rather than allow them to be integrated. Instead of school districts being responsible for devising plans to frustrate the *Brown* decision, a state board was now created for this purpose. Beginning in 1956 until the confrontation at Little Rock in 1957–58, "massive resistance" prevailed throughout the South. But a powerful reaction among white parents against having their children's schools closed, along with federal court decisions demanding that they be opened, reversed this strategy of "massive resistance" and brought it to a halt by the end of 1960.

The South's proclivity for taking a rigid stand at the outer limits had been invoked yet again. And it would reappear on one further occasion—in the early 1960s, when state universities were being pressured to admit black students. State governors once more urged resistance, and two of them in particular, Ross Barnett of Mississippi and George Wallace of Alabama, gained considerable publicity, if not notoriety, because of their confrontational tactics. The spotlight had moved away from Congress and focused instead on states and their governors where closing schools, rather than closing off debate, was the flashpoint of southern resistance.

Although the South's congressmen had been pushed aside by the schools crisis, they were far from immobilized. As qualified compliance changed to "massive resistance," Harry Byrd and Strom Thurmond, senators from Virginia and South Carolina, circulated a Declaration of Constitutional Principles endorsing interposition and noncompliance. Their fighting words were toned down somewhat in the final version of the "Southern Manifesto" of March 1956, which was signed by all of the region's senators save three, and all of its 106 representatives except seventeen, almost all from Texas. In its final form, the declaration still accused the Supreme Court of "clear abuse of judicial power," though stopping short of describing the decision as unconstitutional. And it still commended those states that were planning to "resist forced integration by any lawful means," while committing the congressmen themselves "to use all lawful means" to reverse a decision they considered "contrary to the constitution." Although the message of the manifesto was confused and contradictory, the South's congressional delegation was making sure that its role was still central and preeminent.

Concurrent with the southern delegation's cryptic remarks about "massive resistance," a development was under way in Washington that challenged frontally the South's strategy of a frontier and filibuster defense. The increasing salience of civil rights as the schools crisis roiled the southern states put pressure on the Eisenhower administration to take some action. In order to respond to the civil rights issue as well as to shore up the Republicans' support among black voters in the northern cities, the administration formulated its own plan in the form of a civil rights bill. Its thrust was, however, primarily administrative, while its focus was on voting rights, not the protection of civil rights more broadly.

From the outset, Russell and a number of southern senators recognized that a filibuster could fail. First, Republicans were likely to support a moderate bill proposed by a Republican administration. And second, the Southern Caucus might not be able to control four senators—Lyndon B. Johnson and Ralph Yarborough from Texas; and Al Gore, Sr., and Estes Kefauver from Tennessee—who were moderates on many issues, including civil rights. This would reduce its vote to a mere eighteen. Accordingly, the caucus agreed with the recommendation of its chairman to avoid a filibuster and instead try to weaken the bill so that, if it passed, it would probably be palatable to southern whites. Particularly important for Russell's risky and unprecedented maneuver was Lyndon Johnson, who had been the majority leader in the Senate since 1955. Not only was LBJ a protégé of the avuncular Georgian, who saw in him a viable future southern presidential candidate, but the Texan was also a very skillful politician who could cajole reluctant senators to support debilitating amendments to the Republicans' civil rights bill.

Working in tandem, Johnson and Russell produced a bill in 1957 that was so weakened that its passage was not threatening to the South. Title III, which expanded the federal government's authority to integrate schools, was removed, while Title IV was altered significantly so that violators of the law's provisions would receive a trial by jury—which in the South would consist entirely of whites—instead of a bench trial before a federal judge. The amended bill passed both houses. A filibuster was forbidden because it would have undermined the negotiating, participatory stance that the two men had pursued so purposefully in order to gut the bill. Yet, because it was still a civil rights bill, even though emasculated, all but four of the South's senators voted against it. They had participated in the legislative process, not for the purpose of enacting a civil rights bill, but solely to protect the South from the initial measure proposed by the administration that was likely to pass. Besides, maybe the northern demand for civil rights legislation could be satisfied with a nominal bill, thereby postponing, or even avoiding altogether, a law that was really dangerous.

Southern hopes that the 1957 act would make further civil rights initiatives unnecessary, at least for the next few years, were soon dashed by the schools crisis in Little Rock and elsewhere. In response, the Eisenhower administration, which was being pressured by civil rights advocates in Congress as well as by the Justice Department, introduced a second measure in late 1959 intended to increase the government's enforcement power. When this new bill became a captive of the Judiciary Committee chaired by James Eastland of Mississippi, Johnson introduced a substitute that soon accrued so many strengthening amendments that the Southern Caucus felt compelled to employ the filibuster in order to defeat it. The resulting debate continued around the clock for two weeks in late February and early March 1960. At this point, cloture was invoked by supporters of the bill, but it failed and the bill died.

Johnson then returned to the administration bill. Under threat of a renewed filibuster, the Senate produced a considerably weakened version of the original proposal that passed 74–18, with the members of the Southern Caucus providing the nay votes. Even though this was a civil rights act, none of its six provisions actually threatened the system of segregation. The measure simply tightened the procedures for administering federal elections and for responding to voters' complaints about being denied the right to vote. Once again, the Southern Caucus, aided by the crucial involvement of Majority Leader Johnson, had allowed a civil rights bill to pass, but only after its members had emasculated it. This time, however, they had employed their threat of a filibuster to weaken the measure, rather than to kill it, a course they had never risked before.

Four years later, the South's senators reverted to the traditional use of their weapon of first resort by wielding the filibuster in order to destroy a civil rights proposal. As the civil rights movement entered its climactic stage in the early 1960s, the Kennedy administration introduced a comprehensive public accommodations measure that, if enacted, would quite possibly end legal segregation in the South. The end-game of the white South's struggle to preserve its system of racial domination had begun, and it would be brought to a conclusion by Lyndon Johnson himself, who had now become president after Kennedy's assassination in November 1963.

Success would contribute significantly to Kennedy's legacy as well as to his own record of accomplishment as president. Besides, Johnson had now become convinced that ending segregation was in the South's best interest. And he himself, an accidental southern president, could play a major rule in bringing about this risky yet crucial change in his region's racial order. Although the bill that Johnson submitted to Congress in January 1964 was far stronger than Kennedy's, it managed nevertheless to garner an overwhelming vote of 290–130 in the House. Support for major civil rights legislation was clearly on the rise. But passage in the Senate was far from assured because the measure had first to overcome a filibuster. Supporters of the bill knew they had the fifty-one votes necessary for passage, but they were not at all sure of the extra sixteen needed to end debate, that is, the two-thirds of the Senate's membership required to cut off a filibuster.

And a filibuster was all but certain. The southerners had to defeat this bill, rather than weaken it and thereby make it more likely to pass. Their efforts in 1957 and 1960 had been intended to delay the inevitable. But the 1964 bill *was* the inevitable. And once it became the order of business in the Senate, Richard Russell announced definitively, "Now, we begin to fight the war."[13] For the next three months, the Senate was embroiled in its longest filibuster ever, which came to a close on 10 June. The vote for closing off debate was 71–29, four more than the required two-thirds. After foiling eleven previous attempts to secure cloture on a civil rights measure, the Southern Caucus had finally met defeat. A week later, the Civil Rights Act was passed with a similarly conclusive vote of 73–27, with five Republicans and one Democrat (Robert Byrd of West Virginia) joining twenty-one southerners in opposition to passage.

When it was all over, some participants wondered why Russell had pursued such a risky strategy and so lost everything. Even Hubert Humphrey, the leader of the Senate's Democratic supporters of the bill, found the southerners' tactics surprising. Since Russell had acknowledged privately that the bill was almost certain to succeed, why did he not try to soften it, rather than let it pass unamended?[14] But this puzzlement is itself puzzling. Why would the Southern Caucus have acted in any other way? In their moment of extreme crisis and after decades of battling against every hint of a challenge to their system of race relations, there was no point in trying to soften or mitigate the impact of what might well produce the overthrow of segregation. But, more important, a filibuster might actually succeed. The civil rights forces needed votes from twenty Republicans, only half of whom were on board or sympathetic. And these necessary votes could not be obtained without the active involvement of the party's minority leader in the Senate, Everett M. Dirksen of Illinois. He had to round up hesitant Republican senators and reassure them by means of a very wordy, but not substantively different, "substitute" for much of the bill's existing language. As a result, the "Dirksen substitute" and the votes mobilized in support of it clinched the vote for cloture.

But besides the possibility of a filibuster succeeding and the pointlessness of negotiating a less extreme civil rights bill, the tradition of southern resistance to threats like the FEPC, poll-tax repeal, and antilynching legislation had been to use the Senate's venerated practice of "continuous debate" to obstruct and defeat the menacing legislation. This "tried and true" aggressive response had succeeded every time in the past. And if it were not employed at the most critical moment when the South's entire system of racial control was in peril, not just one feature of it as in the past, then southern voters would wonder what was going on and conclude that the struggle was being abandoned without a fight. In that case, the Southern Caucus would almost certainly be blamed for the defeat, whereas defeat after putting up a good fight would be blamed on their opponents. If that were the case, Richard Russell could say, as he did before the final vote on the Civil Rights Act was cast, "No group of men could have worked harder in a nobler cause. Undismayed and unintimidated . . . we have fought the good fight until we were overwhelmed and gagged."[15]

By referring to the vote to end debate on the civil rights bill as, in effect, a silencing of speech about segregation, Russell had brought the debate in Congress over slavery and segregation full circle. In the 1830s, the abolitionists had complained about being "gagged" by the "gag rule" prohibiting debate about slavery; in 1964, the leader of the segregationists in the Senate complained that they were now being "gagged" by the cloture rule that ended discussion of the South's twentieth-century racial system. There can be little doubt that the chairman of the Southern Caucus intended to make that very connection when he used this evocative and historically significant word on this historically significant occasion.

4

The Over-Representation Mechanism

On his deathbed, in March 1850, John C. Calhoun is reported to have exclaimed sadly, "The South, the poor South, what will become of her!" Fourteen years earlier, at the start of the petition fight, he had worried about the southern senators allowing themselves to be divided and distracted "on this, to us, all-momentous question." For, he emphasized, "We are here but a handful in the midst of an overwhelming majority."[1] His younger colleague, James Henry Hammond, with whom Calhoun had launched the 1836 campaign against receiving abolition petitions, described the South very differently in his maiden speech in the Senate in 1858. (Hammond's maiden speeches in both houses were real humdingers—he obviously believed that first impressions are lasting!) This was the speech in which he proclaimed that "Cotton is King" and proceeded to explain that, like all great civilizations, the South relied on "the very mud-sills of society," in this case, its African slaves, "to do the mean duties, to perform the drudgery of life." He concluded this memorable speech with the proud boast that "we, the slaveholders of the South, took our country in her infancy, and after ruling her for sixty out of the seventy years of her existence, we surrender her to you [the free northern states] without a stain upon her honor, boundless prosperity, the wonder and the admiration of the world."[2] Far from a poor and overwhelmed minority, Hammond's slave-owning South had actually run the country, and had run it superbly well.

THE SLAVE POWER

The perception that the South wielded a disproportionate influence within the national government was not confined to Hammond alone, although his image of the nation as a possession of the South since its formation was memorable. Other contemporaries were less exuberant than Hammond, but their point was similar. The South may have been a numerical minority, since its white population had been dwindling until it was only a third of the national total in 1860. Yet its representation in Washington was far greater. In a speech at the height of the secession crisis, Alexander H. Stephens urged his fellow Georgians to remain in the Union, where southerners had for so long held a greater share of the major offices than northerners. The region's experience had hardly been that of a persecuted minority: "We have had a majority of the Presidents chosen from the South; as well as the control and management of most of those from the North. We have had sixty years of Southern Presidents to their twenty-four." In addition, eighteen Supreme Court justices had been southerners to the North's eleven. Twenty-four presidents *pro tem* of the Senate to their eleven. Twenty-three speakers of the house to the North's twelve. A fourteen-to-five majority of attorneys general. Ambassadors ran eighty-six to fifty-four in the South's favor. And finally, the "vast majority" of higher offices in the army and navy had been held by southerners, while "more than two-thirds" of the 3,000 "clerks, auditors and comptrollers" employed in the executive branch "over the last fifty years" were from the South.[3]

Southerners like Stephens and Hammond were not alone in crediting the South with disproportionate representation in the federal government, and therefore greater influence over it. Northerners such as Senator

William Henry Seward of New York made the case over and over again, and often in excruciating detail, that southerners were over-represented and had been allowed to exert more influence than they deserved. By the 1850s, leading figures in the Free Soil and Republican parties had coined a new term, "the Slave Power," and were sprinkling it liberally in their speeches. As a description of the excessive number of important offices that the representatives of the southern states commanded, it was probably accurate. Several scholarly studies of the executive branch and of members of Congress and the Supreme Court during the antebellum era have provided compelling quantitative data to this effect. During these five or so decades, the population of the southern states dropped from a half to a third of the nation, even though the number of slave states more than doubled. Nevertheless, between 50 and 60 percent of the executive appointments made by John Adams, Jefferson, and Jackson were from the South. Half of the major executive and diplomatic positions from 1787 to 1860 went to southerners. And between 1788 and 1850, southerners controlled the presidency for fifty of these sixty-two years, the House speakership for forty-one years, and the chairmanship of the House Ways and Means Committee for forty-two.[4] In this descriptive and statistical sense, there was, as Eric Foner once acknowledged, "much truth" to the notion of southern political power.[5]

But the term "Slave Power" was not purely descriptive; it was pejorative. Coined by the southerners' opponents, it was intended to implicate them in a devious and deceitful maneuver to acquire influence that they did not deserve and for purposes that were considered nefarious. Some who employed the term went even further and expanded it to "the Slave Power Conspiracy," charging that southern influence had been achieved as a result of an insidious plot to manipulate and deceive. Whether used to describe an undesirable political reality or a conspiracy, "Slave Power" was an adverse characterization. This was quite unlike another term coined a half century later to describe another instance of the southerners' ability to coordinate and deploy their political power successfully. This time, the phrase was "the Solid South." It was invented by southerners themselves, who employed it unhesitatingly and even proudly. "Solid South" was, therefore, quite unlike "Slave Power," which was created by northerners who were worried about the South's influence and wanted to alert their supporters about what southerners were up to.

I intend to return later to "the Slave Power" and examine how the slaveholding South maximized its political assets to obtain considerable influence in the antebellum period. But let me first discuss the single aspect of the slave South's political power that provoked its enemies most. This was the "three-fifths clause." Located in Article I, section II, of the U.S. Constitution, which delineates the legislative branch and, in the process, apportions representation in the lower house of Congress, the clause provided that slaves be included as part of the population on which representation was to be based. As a result, the number of representatives the slaveholding states were entitled to was increased by what amounted to an extra third. According to the historian, Leonard Richards, the method of calculating the slave ratio gave the South an extra fourteen congressional districts in 1793, seventeen in 1812, and twenty-five in 1833, and around twenty thereafter.[6] If the slave population grew, either through importation or by natural increase, then the representation in the House of the slaveholding states expanded accordingly. Since the slave population did grow, almost entirely through natural increase after the ending of the slave trade in 1808, the South benefited from the built-in political reward the clause generated.

That payoff was not confined to the South's quota of representatives in Congress, either. For the number of electors that a state was entitled to in the Electoral College consisted of its total delegation in Congress, that is, its two senators and its growing number of representatives. Also affected by the number of congressmen that a state possessed was the size of its vote, and therefore its influence, within the political party caucuses in Washington. In particular, this applied to the Democratic caucus, where most southerners were to be found after 1830. They had been concentrated in the Jeffersonian Republican caucus before that.[7] With their growing number of extra representatives, the southern states' influence in Congress, in the Electoral College, and in the Democrats' party caucus also increased.

Of course, the delegates at Philadelphia in 1787 could not have imagined that their "three-fifths clause" would give so much to the slaveholding states. Most delegates, even some southerners, did not think slavery was likely to last much longer, and they certainly did not anticipate its spreading westward as far as Texas, and even beyond after the War against Mexico. Moreover, all the delegates lived in states where slavery had existed prior to the Revolution. Those states north of Maryland had abolished the practice during the war and just after it, but slaves still lived in New England and the middle states because they had not abolished slavery completely but had provided for its gradual phasing out. Thus, there were still slaves in New York as late as the 1840s. Slavery was therefore less threatening or unfamiliar to the Framers than it would later appear to those living outside the South by the time abolitionism arose forty years later.

The writers of the Constitution were therefore creatures of their own time, not omniscient prophets. Moreover, they were grappling with a quite mundane political difficulty when they decided to include slaves in the ratio of representation.[3] The question at issue was the manner in which the two houses of Congress were to be apportioned. And the arrangement that was eventually reached consisted of two parts, namely, equal representation for the states in the upper house, the Senate, with representation in the lower house based on the population of each state, and therefore proportional and unequal.

But this "Great Compromise" at the center of the debates in the convention raised a further question—what constituted "the population"? The delegates had already rejected the possibility of basing representation on voters because that would encourage each state to qualify as many voters as it could in order to outmatch its rivals. To the Founders, that option was unwise and undignified and, even worse, it might lead rapidly to universal suffrage, that is, democracy. Like political parties, democracy was not something to be encouraged. On the other hand, they had also rejected the possibility of basing representation on property because the wealthier states would then have greater representation. This basis was invidious, they thought, and besides how would the property basis be determined—fixed assets, liquid assets, or both, and so on?

Those decisions left population as the only possible grounds. And if that were so, then nonvoters would have to be included. Since everyone agreed that women and children who were dependents and outside the body politic were to be included in the population, as they would have to be, then why not the slave population as well? That made pretty good sense, especially since some of the slaveholding delegates wanted it and the purpose of the gathering was to produce agreement, rather than to right all the possible wrongs within the new nation at this precarious moment of its creation. All the same, unlike women and children who would each count as one whole person, even newly born infants, slaves were to be reduced to a fraction. And the reason for this was, not because they were less than human, but because they were property as well as human beings.

Their anomalous status as human property produced a strange fraction, not the more familiar halves, quarters, and thirds, but three-fifths, or 60 percent. This fraction had been proposed by James Madison in 1783 in assigning liability for taxes to each state according to its population, slave as well as free. The slaveholding members of Congress under the Articles of Confederation had accepted it as a suitable proportion. When some members of the Philadelphia convention recalled this formula of 1783 and suggested it as the method for determining slave population in 1787, they also made direct taxes follow the three-fifths requirement. "More representation, more taxes" was therefore the *quid pro quo.* As it turned out, however, taxes levied by the future federal government would be raised indirectly throughout the nineteenth century, namely, through duties on imports. Consequently, the slaveholders increased their representation but did not have to pay for it by having their personal taxes raised.[9]

The three-fifths clause had followed inexorably from the predictable decision to base representation in the lower house on population. Nevertheless, the formula was soon denounced as a strange concoction cooked up to appease the slave owners, a free gift without any reciprocal payment in the form of taxes, in effect, a "corrupt bargain." Moreover, this bonus was not a one-time gain, but a gift that kept on giving for as long as the slave population increased. And this supposed deal lay at the foundation of the South's unmerited and excessive over-representation within the central government and the national party system. Whatever power the southern slaveholders wielded was tainted, not just by the system of human bondage that their power was intended to protect, but by its origins in the very constitutional fabric and governmental framework of the nation.[10]

The three-fifths clause certainly benefited the slaveholding states. John Adams and his son, John Quincy (pronounced "Quinzy"), could both testify to the advantages it bestowed on their southern presidential opponents, Jefferson and Jackson respectively. In the 1800 election, John Adams lost by eight votes, but it was his poor showing in the South that was to blame. A Federalist newspaper estimated that, in the Electoral College, "the black representation from the SLAVE COUNTRY amounted to 15; so that the negroes turned the majority, and actually put in the President."[11] Indeed, because of this, his detractors called Jefferson the "Negro President." Twenty-eight years later, John Quincy could attribute his defeat by Andrew Jackson to the slaveholding South's over-representation in the Electoral College. Jackson's 400,000 or so votes in the northern states provided him with 73 electoral votes, whereas his roughly 200,000 votes in the South netted him 105. Nationwide, Adams lost 178–83, even though he won 44 percent of the vote. Clearly, the padded southern representation was to blame.[12]

The tainted three-fifths clause that increased southerners' representation in the House was not, however, the only mechanism they manipulated in order to increase their political power. The Senate, with its organizing principle of equal state representation, proved even more useful than the House. Prior to the Missouri crisis, senators had operated on an informal, but accepted, formula for admitting territories to statehood, a process aimed at ensuring parity between the increasingly rivalrous sections. Since there was no accepted definition of when a territory was sufficiently settled and populated to qualify for admission as a state, admitting them in pairs had seemed to be a less problematic criterion. The Missouri Compromise of 1820, admitting slave Missouri in exchange for free Maine, seemed to confirm this previously tacit agreement. But in practice, over the next twenty-five years three slave states and only one free state entered the Union, giving the South a clear majority. As a result, the South obtained an advantage that ensured the region's control, especially when supplemented by the usual four or five northern senators like Ninian Edwards and Jesse Thomas who were southern-born Illinoisans still sympathetic to the South. This pattern would continue into the 1850s, even after two more free states were added, Iowa in 1846 and Wisconsin in 1848. During the two critical decades of the 1840s and 1850s, southerners could rely on the Senate, even with the help of just a handful of northern sympathizers, to defeat unpalatable measures. Among these were the anti-slavery Tallmadge amendment to the first Missouri bill in 1819 and the Wilmot proviso in 1846. At the same time, legislation important to the South could obtain Senate approval, such as the Kansas-Nebraska Act in 1854 and the Kansas statehood bill of 1858 containing the proslavery Lecompton constitution (though the bill was later defeated in the House, where Stephen Douglas's break with Buchanan over the measure made passage impossible).[13]

Despite the underlying assumption of parity in the number of free and slave states, a profound inequality was built into the structure of representation. Time after time, the slave states that were admitted were no longer large states as Virginia had been during the first few decades after the Revolution, but states with populations far smaller than those of the northern states entering the Union. On average, they contained just 63,000 free inhabitants compared to the 160,000 of the nonslave territories. As a result, a system of representation based on state equality and population inequality which was intended to benefit small states still did so, except that these small states were now more accurately categorized as slave states.[14]

Within each chamber of Congress, the South took advantage of institutional mechanisms—the three-fifths clause in the House and the state-parity principle in the Senate—to ensure its over-representation and thereby leverage its influence. But there was one other political institution through which the region built up "the Slave Power" so resented by northern politicians. And this was the Democratic Party. In choosing its presidential nominee, Jackson's Democratic Party introduced a new institution, the convention, to replace the caucus that the Republicans had used previously. Almost immediately, the southerners obtained a veto power in the national convention over a nominee not to their liking. In 1836 when Jackson's heir-apparent, Martin Van Buren, was the front-runner, the southerners insisted that, in return for their supporting Van Buren this time, the party's choice in future had to secure at least two-thirds of the delegate vote. On two occasions, they wielded this minority veto power to deny the nomination, first to Van Buren in 1844 and then to Stephen Douglas in 1860. But the very threat of this veto was usually sufficient to deter the party from selecting nominees unacceptable to the South, a pressure to which the Democrats succumbed on a regular, quadrennial basis in the antebellum years.

The other arena where the South exerted disproportionate influence within the Democratic Party was in the legislative branch. From its founding, the party had been predominantly southern in personnel and complexion. In its first decade or so, the Democrats' primary objective was the dismantling of the American system, which was also the southerners' chief preoccupation. As the constitutional lawyer and historian, the late David P. Currie, concluded, in his third volume of *The Constitution in Congress* (2005), "It was the Democrats, led by their southern wing, who killed the American System. . . . Democrats, especially Southern ones, tended to have a deathly fear of federal authority, and they construed it narrowly at every turn."[15] Then, after 1844 when the aggressively expansionist southern president, James K. Polk, took office, the Democrats in Congress tightened their party structure in a way that gave the South even greater control than before. Now it was decided that the party caucus in each house was to select the members of the standing committees and their chairmen. And they would be ranked henceforth by their length of service on the committee, in other words, by seniority. This system of assigning members by seniority and at the behest of the party caucus enabled the southerners to hunker down and dominate the legislative process.

By 1848, southern control of the party's structure in Congress was sufficiently galling to provoke a group of northern Democrats led by Martin Van Buren to leave the party in protest and briefly ally with the new Free Soil Party. In exchange, Van Buren himself accepted the still-small party's presidential nomination. And ten years later, in 1858, George E. Pugh, an Ohio Democrat, complained on the Senate floor about the South's use of the seniority system to dominate the committees. "Your usage is intolerably bad," he admonished the southerners. "It has operated to give Senators from slave-holding states the chairmanship of every single committee that controls the public business of this government. There is not one exception."[16] Of course, by this time, the number of Democratic congressmen from the North had been depleted by the outburst of opposition provoked by Stephen Douglas's Kansas-Nebraska Act and then by the Lecompton constitution, both of which southerners supported, especially Lecompton. At this point, southern Democrats outnumbered their northern colleagues by two to one, 69 seats to 32. Only six years earlier, however, the 1852 elections had returned 92 free-state Democrats and 67 from the slave states. On the eve of secession, therefore, the southerners had an impressive majority in the party's House delegation and caucus, and their control over the body's committee system was overwhelming. How ironic that, possessing this degree of influence, most southern Democrats vowed to destroy the Democratic Party in 1860.[17]

The power of the slaveholding South, "the Slave Power," had not been achieved by a conspiracy or some sleight of hand. It was simply the result of coordinated and unceasing efforts to maximize the region's numbers and its position within the structure of the federal government, primarily through the national Democratic Party. Since the Democrats controlled the presidency and Congress for almost all the thirty years of sectional crisis, the southerners managed to exert considerably more influence than their one-third of the nation's population warranted. And this was supremely ironic, since John C. Calhoun had been convinced that the South should not rely upon parties for protection, but only upon itself and its unity.

Dismissing institutions like political parties as untrustworthy, Calhoun labored, though with little success, to construct *constitutional* formulations that might offer guarantees and security for the region. The first was the right of a state to disobey any federal law it considered hostile by invoking the doctrine of nullification and implementing its accompanying mechanism, the state veto. The second was the acknowledgment of the South as "a concurrent majority" within the nation, rather than as a permanent minority, through the creation of a new institution, the dual executive, one northern, the other southern. But as David Potter explained in his 1968 Fleming Lectures, the South rejected Calhoun's reliance on formal constitutional devices and depended instead on the institutions of government and party. Since institutions are, by nature, functional, the choice of institutional function over constitutional form, to reverse Louis Sullivan's architectural credo that "form follows function," provided a remedy for the South's minority status that Calhoun's theorizing was, in actual practice, unable to supply.

THE SOLID SOUTH

In the space of just two years, from 1858 to 1860, the ascendancy that the South had obtained within the Democratic Party and in the three branches of the national government evaporated, as the anti-slavery, anti-southern Republican Party seized control. A most remarkable and sudden reversal of fortune. Eight years later, after the failure of its attempt to create an independent republic under the control of wealthy, slave-owning white men, the Confederate South was dragged back into the Union. Once again, its political class was confronted with the problem it had faced earlier during the 1850s, namely, how to protect itself from the rest of the country. This time, the region did not try to win control of the central government, since that objective was neither attainable nor necessary. Instead, the South assumed an essentially defensive posture, fending off attacks from the national government and obstructing whatever hostile legislation it produced. The region therefore accepted its minority status and attempted simply to restrict the majority, just as Calhoun had urged. Even though its leaders now accepted Calhoun's recommended mode of operation, they still exploited the existing institutional means available to them, in particular the Democratic Party, a path the Carolinian had actually warned against in the 1840s.

During the sixty or so years following the Civil War, the Democrats were in the minority nationally, exactly the reverse of their dominance in the three decades from 1830 to the late 1850s. The South's strategy was to use this minority party defensively within the national political arena so as to protect its vital interests. Although working through existing parties was not Calhoun's way of defending the South, the postwar strategy was based on the region's acceptance of its minority status and the adoption of obstructionism as the primary tactic, as the Carolinian had recommended.

The strategy of the "Solid South" that evolved during these post–Civil War decades contained at its core a new version of the notorious three-fifths clause. That this novel variant provoked the ire of northerners to a much lesser degree is curious, especially since its impact and benefit were far greater. With the abolition of slavery, the South, which had fought a long and bloody war to save it, received a wonderful and unanticipated reward. It may have been unplanned, but it was certainly undeserved. When southern blacks became free, southern whites were rewarded with the extra two-fifths they had previously been denied. That meant the addition of about a dozen congressmen to the twenty or so they had already gained from the three-fifths clause. To Republican congressmen trying to devise the terms for readmission of the defeated rebels to the Union, this was a gross injustice. One of them, James A. Garfield of Ohio, a Civil War general and future president, expressed the outrage they all felt when he asked: "Shall the death of slavery add two-fifths to the entire power which slavery had when slavery was living? . . . Shall such be the reward of those who did the foulest and guiltiest act which crimsons the annals of recorded time? No, sir; not if I can help it."[18]

To deny the South this unmerited benefit, Congress devised a set of conditions for the defeated South in 1866 that later became the Fourteenth Amendment. Its second clause required the southern states to enfranchise their adult male African American citizens or else have their representation in Congress reduced. This stipulation made the extra representation conditional on providing blacks with the vote. For other reasons besides this particular provision, all the southern states rejected the proposed amendment overwhelmingly. Because of their noncompliance, they were soon saddled with the Reconstruction Act of March 1867. This federal law mandated universal suffrage and, in the process, ensured that a new Republican Party would be voted into office in all the southern states as a prerequisite for their readmission to the Union. Southern representation was now increased by the five-fifths rule, but the beneficiary would be the region's new Republican Party, not the former Confederates. Almost all the region's congressional delegation was now Republican, and all but one of the southern state governments (Virginia was the exception) were under Republican control. The former Confederates had lost the battle over postwar terms for readmission. They were now out of power in their states, and many of them were also disfranchised. Within a decade, however, they had fought their way back and, by means more foul than fair, had regained control of their states. This meant that the southern states were now governed by the Republicans' opponents, the Democrats.

Over the next twenty years, from 1880 to 1900, the southern Democrats proceeded to maintain themselves in power by identifying their party publicly and proudly as "the white man's party." Then, they manipulated and defrauded black voters relentlessly in order to deprive the Republicans of their critically important base of electoral support. Finally, in the 1890s, the Democrats moved aggressively to eliminate black voting altogether by rewriting the voting requirements in their state constitutions so as to make blacks ineligible. Reducing the black vote in the 1880s by informal means, such as electoral fraud and violence, was therefore replaced in the 1890s by a formal and legal device, constitutional disfranchisement, that removed the black vote almost entirely. This meant the end of black voting and therefore of the region's Republican Party as well. Disfranchisement also prevented African Americans from voting in congressional elections, not just at the state level. In fact, disfranchisement was a flagrant denial of the right to vote guaranteed by the Fifteenth Amendment that had been ratified in 1870 during Reconstruction.

This unremitting assault on the constitutionally guaranteed rights of U.S. citizens did not go unobserved by the congressmen from the political party directly affected by it. In 1890, the Republican majority had tried to counter the southern Democrats' efforts to suppress the black vote with a federal elections bill, providing for increased supervision of elections in the South. Unfortunately, this measure failed to pass after the Democrats did something that was quite rare in the Senate during the nineteenth century. They mounted a filibuster against what they denounced as a "force bill." Three years later, the Democrats won control of Congress and, at the behest of the party's dominant southern wing, they proceeded to repeal all the election legislation passed during Reconstruction. The Republicans were appalled that the national government was no longer able to enforce the voting rights guaranteed by the Fifteenth Amendment. But the southern Democrats proceeded to take advantage of the ending of federal supervision of elections. They disfranchised blacks entirely, along with perhaps over a million poor, illiterate whites who could not meet the new qualifications. What would the Republicans do now?

There were just two possible courses of action open to them, and both were tried. The first was to deny congressmen, who were elected from disfranchising states, their seats in the body. This remedy was attempted on several occasions by bringing complaints to the committee on elections in each chamber, claiming that the members in question had been elected unfairly through the rigged process. But this tactic proved unsuccessful. A more plausible response was to reduce the representation of these states in Congress. The Fourteenth Amendment, referred to earlier, had been ratified in 1868 after its initial rejection in 1866. Its second clause provided both the means and the authority to act, because these states had denied the vote to their black voters and so could have their representation reduced proportionally. Furthermore, the year 1901, when the House had to be reapportioned after the 1900 census, presented the occasion and the opportunity for reduction to be imposed. But when two reapportionment bills were introduced, neither contained a provision for reducing the number of congressmen from the four states that had already implemented disfranchisement. Undeterred, a group of Republicans made the case for reduction. Marlin Olmsted of Pennsylvania explained that the electorate had been so devastated in the disfranchising states that about 400,000 voters in Mississippi, North Carolina, South Carolina, and Louisiana elected twenty-seven congressmen, the same number elected by his own state's 900,000 voters.[19] A few years later, the influential black leader, Booker T. Washington, pointed out that John Sharp Williams, the Democratic Leader in the House, was elected in 1902 from a district in Mississippi with 12,000 potential white and 30,000 potential black voters. Yet only 1,493 votes were actually cast in the contest. This was a case of over-representation on a massive scale.[20]

But the deliberations over reapportionment in 1901, the one moment when action was quite appropriate and possible and might deter other states from following the example of these first four, ultimately produced no remedy. A bill intended specifically to reduce southern representation was presented by Edgar D. Crumpacker of Indiana, who, for the next few years, waged an unflagging but lone campaign for reduction, often derided as "Crumpackerism." His bill insisted that the nation punish the disfranchising states by reducing their representation by the same percentage as each state's illiteracy rate. The presumption was that, since no illiterates could meet the educational tests that the new state constitutions had imposed, they had therefore been automatically disfranchised. But, even among Republicans, there was little support for the bill. The issue resurfaced in various forms over the next few years, but it soon became more a gesture than an achievable policy.[21]

There were two reasons for this reluctance to act, even though disfranchisement was a flagrant denial of the right to vote that bestowed enormous political benefits on the southern Democrats. In the first place, reduction proved extremely problematic. As a policy, reducing a state's representation did not stop or reverse disfranchisement; it merely acknowledged it as a fact and punished its perpetrators. And actually, the South's Democrats were prepared to suffer a reduction in the number of congressional seats they held as long as it permitted them to remove blacks from politics within their states and thereby destroy the Republican opposition. Furthermore, as a mechanism, reduction was almost impossible to implement. As John Sharp Williams himself was quick to warn, "Out of the number of people who did not vote, how are you going to determine which of them have not acted because of the educational qualification?"—or, he might have added, because of any of the many voting requirements these constitutions contained.[22] A lot of voters might simply have refused, or forgotten, to pay their poll tax. Perhaps they just chose not to vote. Because the grounds were so difficult to ascertain, Crumpacker decided to avoid the quibbling involved and opt for a general, and easily implemented, criterion. He decided to use a state's illiteracy rate as a reasonable indicator of how much of the previously eligible electorate had been eliminated. Still, it was an arbitrary calculation that would probably have been contested and run into difficulties in the courts.

The second reason for the Republicans' unwillingness to press the issue was contextual. In the Spanish-American War of 1898, the first overseas military conflict since the Civil War, southern and northern soldiers fought side by side. Sectional reconciliation was in the air. And so was a shared feeling of racial superiority among white Americans as the nation assumed a colonial stance in dealing with the indigenous, darker-skinned populations of Cuba and the Philippines. Accordingly, the white South's race problem struck a chord with whites outside the region who understood how difficult it must be to live among so many African Americans. As a practical matter, segregating and disfranchising them seemed a reasonable solution. In this climate, both the president, William McKinley, and the Supreme Court concurred that it was best to be conciliatory and approving, rather than to embark on a destructive and ultimately frustrating attempt to reverse the inexorable, even natural, course of events that was unfolding in the South. McKinley toured Georgia and Alabama in December 1898 but made no mention of the disfranchisement campaigns underway in the region. Meanwhile, the Supreme Court in *Plessy v. Ferguson* in 1896 and *Williams v. Mississippi* in 1898 put the stamp of approval on first segregation and then disfranchisement.[23]

The upshot was, of course, a huge over-representation for the South that lasted for more than a half century. The South had gained congressmen as a result of the freeing of the slaves, something they had broken up the nation to prevent. But when they took away the right to vote, these same southerners kept the extra representation that the more than two million disfranchised black voters had given them. Like the three-fifths clause, the South's disproportionate presence in Congress and the Electoral College was based on a distorted and unwarranted electoral base within the southern states themselves. Interestingly, the over-representation resulting from the three-fifths clause was based on too much population, whereas the over-representation produced by disfranchisement was based on too few voters. And the repercussions of these too few voters went well beyond their impact on congressional representation. The severe reduction of the southern electorate and its wiping out of the voting base of the opposition party gave rise to a one-party system quite different in kind from the pattern of one-party dominance and one-party hegemony that had prevailed in the region in the nineteenth century. The South was now solidly Democratic and, *within* the region, the Democratic Party was virtually unchallenged. *Outside* the former Confederacy, however, the South and its Democratic guardians were far from safe and secure. So, the Solid South as an organized political entity had a task to perform, a mission to accomplish.

In one of the many memorable analogies he invented to depict southern politics in the twentieth century, the distinguished political scientist, V. O. Key, described the Solid South as "the instrument for the conduct of the foreign relations of the South with the rest of the nation."[24] In its role as the region's state department, the Democratic Party identified and presented itself as the Solid South. Its congressional delegation, its presidential electors, and its national convention delegates were all organized as a cohesive unit and committed to a political orthodoxy. In essence, they constituted a united front. And what were they defending? Obviously not everything that existed in the South, because the region contained numerous competing interests and constituencies. No, what they were defending was the South's system of race relations, its white supremacy—which, by the turn of the century, had been forged into a formal system of legalized racial segregation and disfranchisement, often referred to euphemistically as Jim Crow.

With the exception of the unsuccessful federal anti-lynching bills in the 1920s and 1930s and the anti–poll-tax bills of the 1940s, the South's new, legalized system of racial domination went unchallenged. However, during the Second World War and for thirty years after it, the federal counterattack was heavy and almost continuous. Yet the South was well prepared to meet the onslaught. As soon as the region's Democrats had returned to Congress after Reconstruction, they picked up where they had left off before the Civil War and began burrowing into the Democratic party machinery in the House and Senate. Very soon, by 1881 in fact, they dominated the party caucuses in both houses because the southerners were not only the majority among the Democrats—they also acted together. Since the Democrats were in the minority in Congress for all but ten years from Reconstruction to 1932, they tightened the rules governing their House and Senate caucuses so as to ensure party discipline and unity. To this end, in 1903, they made a two-thirds vote in the Senate caucus binding on all members, and this procedure was also adopted in the House caucus by the party leader, Champ Clark, after 1909. The southern majority's ability to control was secured.[25] As soon became evident, most of the flood of legislation enacted by Woodrow Wilson was managed and sponsored by southern committee chairmen, and much of it proved very beneficial to southern agriculture.

The other arena within the Democratic Party where the South could exert its influence was the party's nominating convention. Although its delegates were not a majority, they could still wield the weapon of the two-thirds rule to deny the nomination of any aspirant they did not like. The very existence of that rule dissuaded candidates who could not get southern support from running. And on two occasions, the southern delegates actually prevented candidates with a majority of votes from obtaining the necessary two-thirds. The first occurred in 1912 when southern delegates prevented Champ Clark of Missouri from being nominated, resulting in the selection of Woodrow Wilson, who was much more preferable to the South. Then, in 1924, the southerners kept Alfred E. Smith of New York from being nominated by refusing to cast a single ballot for him. Eight years later, the two-thirds rule was rendered ineffective by the massive increase of northern delegates within the party. Franklin D. Roosevelt did not need the South for his first nomination, nor even for the three reelection campaigns that followed. In 1936, the Democratic Party's national convention repealed the rule.

By then it was a device of no use to the South anyway, since the region was now so outnumbered that it could not control the necessary one-third of the convention delegates. The southerners were therefore left to contemplate the unpleasant and completely unfamiliar reality that they had become a permanent minority within their traditional haven, the national Democratic Party.

Amazingly, however, the power of the South had not been destroyed. It had not even been marginalized. Up until this point, the states of the former Confederacy, along with help from border states like Missouri and West Virginia, had managed to exert considerable influence over the Democratic Party, even though they now contained just 25 percent of the nation's population and an even smaller percentage of its registered voters, a mere 10 percent. But, in the 1930s and thereafter, the southern Democrats could no longer dominate their party. Nevertheless, there was still hope, for they had even bigger fish to fry. They would dominate Congress itself. Still a minority in the nation and now a minority within the Democratic Party, the South held a trump card it could continue to play—Congress's committee system.

While the Democrats were in the minority in Congress, Democratic senators and representatives from the South held ranking positions on most of the powerful standing committees. Now that the Democrats controlled Congress during the New Deal decade, these ranking members would be promoted automatically and would possess the chairmanships and the senior majority positions.[26] In essence, they would run the committees. The rules and regulations of both houses were established during the Progressive Era after the operations of Congress had been decentralized by devolving authority from powerful czars, like Thomas Reed in the Senate and Joseph Cannon in the House, onto the standing committees. Ever since then, the chairmen of these major committees had run Congress.

The committee chairmen controlled the flow of legislation. They decided when, or if, their committees met; they supervised the drafting of the committee's bills; they determined whether to introduce the bills and when; and they handled them once they were being debated on the floor. These same rules of Congress also included the seniority system that made length of service the criterion for moving up the ladder to become ranking minority member or chairman. And the South, with its one-party system and its recognition that experience in Congress gave a member influence and reputation, made sure that its congressmen were reelected, not just once, but over and over again. The longer they served, the more clout they could exert and the more seniority they would accrue. With no rival party in the region to interfere, it was easy to ensure reelection and thereby create a large cadre of powerful senators and representatives skilled at manipulating the procedural machinery of Congress and its committee-based operations.

During the roughly thirty Congresses between 1880 and 1970, most of them after 1932 when the Democrats were in control, southerners were chairmen of almost all of the dozen or so standing committees in the House. They often chaired Banking and Appropriations, but they had almost exclusive control over Judiciary, Armed Services, and Agriculture, the latter a bastion of permanent southern control. Most important of all, they ran the committees on Rules and on Ways and Means. The Rules Committee determined what bills would come to the floor for debate and passage, while Ways and Means functioned as a committee on committees through its role in determining what the membership of committees was to be. Meanwhile, in the Senate, southern domination of the committees was equally impressive. When he came to the upper house in 1948, Paul Douglas, a leading liberal Democrat from Illinois, surveyed the scene gloomily, recounting in his memoirs that, "Of the fourteen Senate committees, no fewer than ten had Southern or pro-Southern chairmen. These included such all-important committees as Finance, Appropriations, Armed Services, Foreign Relations, and Judiciary." But the situation was not all bleak. Douglas acknowledged ironically that "there were two somewhat minor committees upon which the Southern overlords permitted the Northerners to sit; Labor and Public Welfare, and Banking and Currency, [though] the latter during my eighteen years had a Southern chairman." Offsetting these minor lapses in their autocratic rule, the southerners made sure they had complete sway over the major committees, since, as Douglas noted, they would not "content themselves with only the top positions. They would stack the important committees with dominance in depth."[27]

The South's control over the Senate through its committees enabled it to facilitate bills that it favored, and to delay, obstruct, and kill legislation it feared. In this task, the region's senators were aided by three other devices, one formal and institutional and the other two informal. The formal institution most essential to the South's ability to influence legislation in the Senate was the body's cherished procedure known as "continuous debate," or the filibuster, that could only be cut off by a vote of cloture, requiring the concurrence of two-thirds of those present and voting. From 1949 to 1959, closing off debate required an even greater number—two-thirds of the entire membership of the Senate. This device, and even just the threat of it, compelled the Senate to hold back on measures known to be adamantly opposed by the South. These were not only race-related civil rights and voting rights proposals, often derided by the southerners as "force bills," but any bill that the southerners considered threatening to their region's racial order.

To bolster the South's position within the body, an informal mechanism was created in 1938 in order to coordinate opposition to the anti-lynching bill in the 1937–38 session. Chaired initially by Tom Connally of Texas and after 1949 by Richard Russell of Georgia, the previously mentioned Southern Caucus consisted of the twenty-two senators from the former Confederate states, and it met regularly to plan strategy on legislation of particular concern to the region's delegation. With the threat to the southern racial order mounting in the 1940s and 1950s and with the opposition coming increasingly from within the Democratic party caucus that the southerners no longer controlled, a separate and exclusive organization of their own was considered vital.

The other informal asset was the collaboration and support that southerners received from conservative Republicans during these same decades. Although this "conservative coalition" never assumed an organized structure in the form of a caucus or committee, understandings based on mutual aims and fears brought them together. This cooperation began in the wake of FDR's attempt in 1938 to expand the Supreme Court and increase the number of liberals on it, a maneuver disparaged by conservatives as his "court-packing plan." And this bipartisan arrangement, an "undercover alliance on economic matters," as Paul Douglas called it, cohered around the issues of race, labor, and social welfare, which were becoming increasingly important during the Second New Deal and after the Second World War.[28] On legislation favoring labor and the poor, southern Democrats and northern Republicans voted together to ensure its defeat. On race, the Republicans aided the southerners procedurally by opposing cloture votes to cut off debate. Unwilling to take a stance hostile to blacks and in favor of segregation, these midwestern and western Republicans could, however, vote in good conscience to protect the Senate's hallowed principle of "continuous debate." Douglas described this deviousness as a way for the Republicans to "hold the Senate passive, so that the Southerners could anesthetize and put the civil-rights measures to death."[29]

The upshot of these formal and informal mechanisms was what became known as "the Senate Establishment," presided over by the southern Democrats along with their conservative Republican allies. In 1957, a study of this informal institution was published called *Citadel*. The author was a *New York Times* journalist from Texas named William S. White, who was in awe of the system the southerners had built in the Senate and now controlled. Expressing his admiration, he portrayed it as "the South's unending revenge upon the North for Gettysburg."[30]

The control of the southern Democrats over the Senate was the heart of their influence within the legislative branch of the national government. But this was buttressed by their disproportionate leverage in the House of Representatives, where they dominated the committee system as well, while they also deployed the accumulated experience of their inordinate numbers of congressmen so as to play a larger role in the

Democratic party caucus than should have been the case. And the irony of it all was that a regional political elite that had fought unremittingly to limit the authority of the federal government and curb its power was only able to do so because the southerners had worked so hard and so successfully to gain control over that very same national government. This excessive influence within a central government that it denounced and disparaged unceasingly was not merely "unending revenge for Gettysburg." It was a paradox, a contradiction, at the very heart of the South's political practice and its political history for almost two centuries.

5

The Dismantling of the Southern Political Tradition

Almost fifty years have now passed since the passage of the Civil Rights Act of 1964 and the Voting Rights Act of 1965. Together, these two federal laws brought to an end the South's system of legalized racial domination that had segregated and disfranchised the region's African American population. The phasing out of this official system was accompanied by the dismantling of the political practices and mechanisms that had protected and defended it, namely, the southern political tradition, which had arisen in the age of slavery and had reached its fullest expression, its zenith, in the Solid South of the Jim Crow era, from the 1890s to the 1960s.

. . .

The most important of the southern political tradition's three component parts was the one-party paradigm. It was challenged frontally by the Voting Rights Act, whose objective was the complete re-enfranchisement of black voters who were still being harassed and denied access to the vote, despite the repeal of the poll tax in 1964 and the provisions for black voting in the civil rights acts of 1957, 1960, and 1964. The Voting Rights Act contained three basic provisions. First, it rejected as ineffective the lengthy process of bringing voting rights cases before the courts and, instead, took a far more immediate and direct route by suspending all literacy and other disfranchising "devices" for five years in those states and counties where less than half of the eligible voters had voted in the 1964 election. It also provided a "triggering mechanism" applicable to the states "covered" by the law (five Deep South states, plus Virginia and parts of North Carolina), whereby federal registrars, not just observers or monitors as in the past, were to be dispatched to those electoral districts where registering to vote was being obstructed. This mechanism was triggered whenever twenty citizens residing in an electoral district requested the registrars, as long as the U.S. attorney general considered it necessary. And finally, section 5 required that any new voting laws or ordinances had to be submitted for prior approval, or "pre-clearance," by the civil rights division of the Justice Department.

Within a few years, black registration in the seven southern states covered by the new law had increased dramatically, from 24.4 percent to 60.7 percent in 1969. By 1970, black voters in the South numbered 3.4 million compared to 1.5 million in 1960. And this number grew to 5.6 million by 1984. Automatically, an increase of this size created a critical mass of new voters who now needed a party to vote for. Ironically, the most likely one was the Democratic Party, the party of white supremacy, which had monopolized southern politics since the beginning of the twentieth century. Because the national Democratic Party had been the driving force behind the legislative campaign for civil rights as well as the enactment of the 1964–65 legislation, blacks gravitated naturally toward the Democrats. Their preference was particularly understandable and rational, since the Republicans' standard bearer in the 1964 presidential election, Senator Barry M. Goldwater, had made clear to voters that he had been wholeheartedly opposed to the Civil Rights Act and had voted against it in July, just a few months earlier.

With the South's one-party system collapsing, the two major parties had now to move quickly to take advantage of the changing situation. What soon emerged was a reorganization and realignment of the region's political parties. Both parties would need to reinvent and reorganize themselves, not just the Democrats. Since the five million black voters were already moving solidly into the Democratic column, the Republicans had to figure out, and soon, how they could become a viable force in the region. Instead of competing for the black vote, which they had little chance of obtaining, the Republicans calculated that their best hope, and it was a very realistic one, was to appeal to angry or alienated white Democrats to leave their party and become founding members of the Republicans' new presence and new organization in the South.

These two parties therefore embarked on a struggle to reinvent themselves. In effect, each had to become what amounted to a new party. The Republicans had to become the party of choice for whites, who had to be enticed away from the previously hegemonic Democratic Party. And the Democrats had to keep as many of their white supporters as possible while absorbing almost all of the newly enfranchised black voters. In practical terms, the Republicans had to forge an overwhelmingly white party that would almost certainly be conservative in sentiment and policy, or else it would never attract the Democrats' traditional support among the region's segregationists. At the same time, the Democrats themselves would have to create a biracial party consisting of a majority who were white and probably conservative, and a minority who were black and almost certainly liberal. To put it bluntly, both had to pursue a "southern strategy" in order to become viable in the South after 1865, and these very different courses of action were the strategies they in fact pursued. No matter how these two parties reconstituted themselves, the South's political system had to undergo a reorganization that was bound to be transformative.

On the night after he signed the Civil Rights Act of 1964, Lyndon Johnson looked over the headlines in the next day's newspapers and confided to his aide, Bill Moyers, that they had just "delivered the South to the Republican Party for your lifetime and mine."[1] The Republicans would simply win over the Democrats' segregationist white support and replace it as the South's only party. But, on this prediction, Johnson's customary political savvy let him down, for the Republicans did not take over right away. In fact, it was not until thirty years later, in the mid-1990s, that they would secure a majority of the region's congressional delegation and even longer before they made much headway in the South's state legislatures.

The Democrats' task of building, and then holding together, a biracial coalition, with part of it probably quite conservative and the other liberal, was clearly the more difficult task. The South had not experimented with a biracial party since as far back as Reconstruction and, ever since then, it had fought desperately against the recurrence of such a calamity. So, given the difficulty the Democrats faced in their remaking of themselves, why was it that the Republicans took so long to become established?

Although there were several contributing elements, the explanation lies primarily in the resilience of the region's Democratic Party as an effective political organization and a respected regional institution. The Democrats had been the only party in all but a few states, such as Tennessee, Virginia, and North Carolina, for almost a hundred years. As the party organization that had defended the region from external threats, it commanded white southerners' loyalty and support. And its continuing institutional influence and experience provided the means for candidates to run for office and obtain financing and organizational endorsement and support. By comparison, the Republican Party's electoral apparatus lacked public acceptance and campaign experience. To put it succinctly and colloquially, the Democrats had been "the only game in town" for decades, while the Republicans were "the new kid on the block."

Besides its reputation and influence at the local and state level, the Democratic Party still controlled the region's delegation in Congress and would continue to do so in the House until 1994 and in the Senate until 2000. Furthermore, those representatives and senators were politicians who possessed experience and power through the seniority system and their continuing domination of the standing committees in both houses. As before, the South benefited immensely from its influence over policy and appropriations in Washington, especially since the Democrats had majorities in both houses of Congress during all but six of the thirty years (1981–87, when the Senate went Republican during Reagan's presidency) after the passage of the Voting Rights Act. The Democrats' continuing institutional power and presence, within the South and within Congress, served therefore as a considerable brake on the rise of the southern Republican Party—a phenomenon that has been characterized rather graphically by the distinguished southern political scientists, Earl and Merle Black, as "the Democratic Smother."[2]

By the early 1990s, however, the ability of "the Democratic Smother" to hold back the rising Republicans was weakening. The three consecutive terms of a Republican presidency from 1980 to 1992—of Ronald Reagan, who was popular in the South, and of his successor, George H. W. Bush—had helped establish the party in the region. Also beneficial to the Republicans were the significant demographic changes in the South during the 1970s and 1980s, as suburbs had proliferated and were filling up with young managers and professionals who had migrated from the Rust Belt to the Sun Belt. They voted Republican, just like suburbanites elsewhere in the country during those decades. Sensing their opportunity in 1994, a congressional election year when the Republicans had a good chance of winning control of Congress, southern Republicans made their region a crucial element in the party's campaign strategy. If they could carry those districts that George Bush Sr. had won in 1992, along with a number of "open seats" that were not being contested by sitting congressmen, they could very likely win a majority of the South's House delegation and even control the House itself (if they won the election, the new Speaker of the House would be Newt Gingrich of suburban Atlanta). The outcome was a decisive victory for the Republicans. They turned a 176–258 disadvantage into a 230–204 majority, with the South's Republican margin shifting from a deficit of 39–77 to a 64–61 majority.

The southern Republicans' victory in the 1994 congressional elections was clearly a breakthrough. Over the next six years, they increased their majority so that, by 2000, their share of the region's congressional delegation stood at 57 percent, while their proportion of the South's Senate seats had risen from 32 percent in 1992 to 59 percent. In addition, they were beginning to make inroads into the state legislatures by 2000, winning both chambers in two states and splitting them in two others. No longer could the reordering of the South's parties be dismissed as merely a "split-level realignment" that was confined to the presidential level only. For the Republicans were now extending their control into Congress and the state assemblies. With the party controlling the presidency as well as both houses of Congress after 2000, the specter of a dominant Republican majority loomed, causing some to wonder whether the Republicans might now be so dominant that they would reinstate a one-party South. But then the election of Barack Obama in 2008, which was accompanied by a Democratic revival in the South and the nation that same year, seemed to indicate that such an eventuality was unlikely.

Two years later, however, in the midterm elections of November 2010, the South's Republicans came back forcefully, winning all the Senate seats that were being contested and increasing their numbers in the House. But most significant were the state-level results. Republicans now held nine of the eleven governorships and both houses of the state legislature in seven of the eleven states (Virginia was split and three others were closely contested). This means that the South's Republicans have finally established themselves at the state level, not just in Congress. Exactly what this portends for the future is hard to tell because American politics has become so volatile, with vast swings occurring over the course of the past three national elections in 2006, 2008, and 2010. But almost certainly, the Republican Party is ascendant in the South at present. While the Republicans may not remain so dominant for long, one thing is clear. The South is not a one-party region anymore, and its politics is not, in any systematic fashion, essentially different from the other regions, or even the country as a whole.

. . .

Just as the South's rigid one-party politics has been phased out, the second element in the southern political tradition, the over-representation mechanism, has also been dismantled. This mechanism was not eliminated as a direct result of the civil rights legislation of the 1960s, although the necessity for its existence as an instrument for protecting the South's racial system had been removed. The region is no longer over-represented because of two other developments within the federal government that brought about the demise of this political distortion that had conferred significant benefits on the South, within the region itself as well as in Congress.

The first of these initiatives arose within the judicial branch contemporaneously with the civil rights movement. While it drew on the ideas of equal rights and justice that animated the civil rights movement, the "representation revolution," as it has been called, took place in the courts, culminating in a series of far-reaching decisions by the U.S. Supreme Court between 1962 and 1964 during Earl Warren's term as chief justice. The two pivotal cases were *Baker v. Carr* (1962) and *Reynolds v. Sims* (1964). In taking cases like these, the Court was breaking new ground by adjudicating suits that challenged the judicial authority of state legislatures in determining their own basis of representation.

Prior to these decisions, state legislatures throughout the United States were operating under systems of representation that had not been changed for decades, many of them not since the early twentieth century, despite enormous shifts in the size and distribution of the population during the intervening decades. As a result, legislatures were severely malapportioned, with rural areas enjoying excessive representation, while cities and especially the new suburbs were woefully underrepresented. Yet these state legislatures seemed congenitally incapable of rectifying this patently unjust, unequal, and obsolete state of affairs. So, the Court decided, over the objections primarily of Justices Felix Frankfurter and John Marshall Harlan, to "enter the political thicket" and compel a state to reapportion its legislature according to the principle of "one person, one vote," instead of continuing to allow residents of one district to have significantly more representation than those of another. If votes weighed more heavily, i.e. counted more, in one district over another, this was discriminatory, so the Court determined, and therefore contrary to the equal protection clause of the Fourteenth Amendment.

In the landmark decisions that ensued, the Court avoided its mistake in *Brown v. Board of Education* by insisting on a deadline for compliance, instead of *Brown*'s vague suggestion of implementation "with all deliberate speed." By the end of the 1960s, the gross disparities in all the state legislatures had, to a remarkable degree, been eliminated, and the electoral districts were now reapportioned as fairly as possible. As the political scientists, Stephen Ansolabehere and James M. Snyder, Jr., have concluded, "By the beginning of the 1970s, equal representation of population had become a new fact of political life." Furthermore, redistricting soon became habitual, as the states all opted to redraw their legislative districts, both state and congressional, every decade after a new census was reported.[3]

The effect of the "representation revolution" on the South was dramatic, because rural areas had long been the backbone of the Democratic Party that dominated the region since the century began. And through the over-representation of these districts, the party had obtained far more elected officials than they would otherwise have been entitled to. Furthermore, the Democrats had benefited even more in those rural areas where blacks were numerous because these districts were over-represented twice. First, because they were rural and, second, because adult male blacks were counted in the population but were not allowed to vote. As northern Republican congressmen pointed out at the time, disfranchisement increased the value of the white Democrats' vote enormously. When the South's Democrats disfranchised black voters, they should, at the very least, have been penalized by having their representation reduced.

The effect of reapportionment on the Democratic Party in the late 1960s and thereafter is, however, difficult to ascertain because the parties were beginning to change and realign at the same time that the redistricting was occurring. Many of the rural Democrats who had been over-represented were now voting Republican, while the changing Democratic Party was looking to the growing cities of the region for support among liberal-to-moderate whites and liberal blacks. On balance, the Republicans gained from the increased representation of the suburbs and lost from the reduced influence of the rural vote, while the Democrats gained from the greater representation of the cities and, to some extent, of the suburbs too. Whichever party improved its relative position as a result of the redistricting, a fairer system that represented the population of the region more accurately was surely an improvement overall that benefited the South and its two fluctuating and realigning parties.

The issue of representation surfaced in another context during the 1980s and 1990s when the under-representation of African American voters became a matter of concern. To guard against attempts by states to limit the impact of the newly enfranchised black voters by rearranging their election laws, section 5 of the Voting Rights Act had included a pre-clearance clause that required states to obtain federal approval of any changes in their election laws that might impede black voting or registration. Rather than actually trying to prevent blacks from voting, which would have been too obvious in its attempt to frustrate the intentions of the Voting Rights Act, states had resorted instead to diminishing the impact of black votes by rearranging apportionment, thereby diluting the vote. This section 5 has in particular made it necessary to renew the Voting Rights Act many times beyond its original five years. Renewal has occurred on four occasions—in 1970, 1975, 1982, and 2006.

Another aspect of black under-representation was evident in the virtual absence of black congressmen among the region's one hundred or so districts in the 1970s. To rectify this alarming deficiency, efforts were made in the late 1980s, and especially after the 1990 redistricting, to concentrate the African American vote in such a way that black voters would have a good chance of electing a black congressman to represent them. African American organizations as well as the Democratic Party pushed for this outcome, with the result that a number of black-majority districts were created in each state. Consequently, twelve black congressmen were elected from the South in 1992, an improvement over just Andrew Young of Georgia, Barbara Jordan of Texas, and Harold Ford of Tennessee in the 1970s.

But there may have been a cost in generating these twelve representatives, because the Democratic Party invariably lost most, if not all, of the remaining districts in the state. Since the districts adjoining the black-majority one had necessarily become more heavily white, they were therefore easier for the Republicans to carry. In fact, Republicans in the civil rights division of the Justice Department during the Reagan years had been actively involved in helping to create black-majority districts for this very reason, namely, the calculation that they would produce more districts that the Republicans could win. The net effect of the formation of these black-majority districts is not clear. Some political scientists think that the Democrats have probably lost overall. Although the black congressmen who won in the black-majority districts have all been Democrats, the party lost seats elsewhere because the districts were no longer sufficiently black, and therefore no longer safely Democratic. Others point out that the Democrats lost most of those seats because of strong electoral trends toward the Republicans that existed independently of the impact of the black-majority districts on the Democrats' prospects. They maintain that the Republicans would have won those seats, and others, anyway. But one thing is certain. Without these black-majority districts, very few black congressmen would have been elected at all. Yet the Voting Rights Act clearly intended to give blacks, not just the vote, but the ability to elect people of their own choosing to represent them in Congress and in their state legislatures.[4]

The other arena where the South was over-represented prior to the 1960s was in Congress itself. There, southern Democrats exerted excessive influence within their own party as well as within the committee system that managed the business of the House and Senate. In the late 1940s and early 1950s, a small group of northern liberals in the Democratic Party, notably Paul Douglas of Illinois and Eugene McCarthy and Hubert Humphrey of Minnesota, had become conspicuous because they decided to challenge the South's dominance. They tried to push the southerners aside and cajole the Democratic Party into recognizing civil rights as the main issue that confronted the nation and the party in the contest with the Soviet Union during the Cold War. At the same time, they tried to weaken the committee system by changing the procedures of the all-important Rules Committee in the House so as to diminish the power of its chairman, Howard W. Smith of Virginia. But the southern Democrats were so entrenched and the institutions of Congress so resistant to change that virtually nothing was achieved.[5]

A decade elapsed before the Solid South's hegemony encountered serious challenge. Two related developments contributed to what turned out to be a showdown. Both were in fact generated from outside Congress. The first was the changing composition of the House as a result of the "representation revolution." Throughout the country, including the South, increasing numbers of representatives from suburban and urban districts were being sent to Congress, and they were less conservative in attitude as well as dissatisfied with, even hostile to, the old ways and values that had permeated the House for decades. They were soon joined by newly elected members who had been shaped by the iconoclastic values of the 1960s and were unwilling to submit to the hierarchical structure of Congress or to all-powerful committee chairmen.

The second development also arose from the critical spirit of the 1960s. Around 1970, print and television media were becoming hostile toward the nation's institutions and were not just reporting the news but probing below the surface of events and engaging in "investigative journalism." In addition, citizens' advocacy organizations like Common Cause and Ralph Nader's Congress Watch were demanding that Congress mend its ways and reform itself. As a result, there was growing pressure outside Congress for structural reform of the institution, not just for the limitation of southern power over its committees and its legislation.[6]

Over the next five years, 1970–75, congressional reform was achieved.[7] In 1970, the Legislative Reorganization Act opened up committee hearings to the public and to radio and television, while also requiring committee votes to be recorded. Both of these innovations prevented chairmen from running their committees in secret and getting legislation enacted without input or criticism from the membership. After the 1972 elections, in which congressional reform had been a significant issue, a series of measures was introduced by the increasingly confident reformers in the House. These initiatives aimed at involving the party leaders in the legislative process, so as to take lawmaking out of the control of the committee chairmen. And they produced results. The Democratic caucus required chairmen to be voted on at the beginning of each session, and the major party leaders were to be members of the Ways and Means Committee, which would appoint chairs and members of the standing committees. Also, subcommittees were to be given some influence over the committees from which they had been formed. Finally, meetings of committees, not just the hearings they held, were to be open to the public and the media.

Significant though these reforms of party procedures were, the chairmen still had considerable power. It was another development occurring outside Congress, the Watergate crisis of 1972–74, that provided the opportunity to bring the chairmen to heel. Although Richard Nixon and his actions that had produced this constitutional crisis were the focus, the 1974 midterm elections were, in effect, a referendum on Washington and its less than admirable ways of conducting itself. The young and politically inexperienced cohort of seventy-five freshmen members were angered by the recent revelations about how the political establishment ran things, and they vowed to take matters into their own hands. In a dramatic maneuver, they formed a "new members caucus" and proceeded to interview the committee chairmen to determine whether they should retain their powerful positions in the new Congress. Three of them, all southerners in fact, made bad impressions and were removed by the precocious novices. And the leadership of the Democratic majority upheld their verdicts. All of these actions since 1970 were so dramatic that, together, they effectively ended the twentieth-century reign of the committee system. And the collapse of the committee system that was based on seniority and despotic chairmen also meant that the domination of the southerners was now over.

▪ ▪ ▪

The third, and final, component of the southern political tradition was the frontier and filibuster defense. Unlike the other two elements in this tripartite tradition, this last one was not so much a structure as a strategy and a weapon. By deciding to treat as a lethal threat any action that looked like a challenge to its systems of slavery and segregation, southern political leaders were selecting a strategy of no compromise and no delay by throwing down the gauntlet at the outset and then standing firm and resolute. This strategy of resisting at the frontier—at the first line of defense instead of taking a stand at a later, and perhaps more obviously consequential, point in the contest—was the course of action pursued by southerners in Congress in defense of their region's racial order.

The weapon they chose for implementing this approach, the Senate filibuster, was not available to them in the nineteenth century. It was a procedure that had not been given much consideration in the Senate and was invoked on very few occasions. And besides, the slaveholding southerners had sufficient votes in the Senate before 1860 that, with the support of the border slave states and of a reliable coterie of northern Democrats ("doughfaces" was the pejorative term for them), they had the capability of defeating any threatening legislative initiative in the Senate.[8] But in the next century the segregationist states of the South were in a clear minority, and the filibuster was the best way to protect their racial order from any legislation they deemed dangerous. Often, the mere threat of endless debate was enough to prevent a vote on a measure, while a vote to end debate required an insurmountable two-thirds majority after the cloture rule was introduced in 1917. So this amalgam of frontier strategy and filibuster weapon served the South in its long struggle over 150 years to protect its two successive systems of racial discrimination and domination.

Naturally, the frontier and filibuster defense was no longer needed once the systems they were protecting had been brought to an end. In the case of slavery, defeat in the war to preserve the South and its system of slavery, coupled with the Emancipation Proclamation and the Thirteenth Amendment to the U.S. Constitution, destroyed the institution. A century later, segregation was effectively abolished by two pieces of federal legislation, the civil rights and voting rights acts. Unlike the South's one-party politics and its over-representation, both of which assumed an institutional and structural form and would fade out gradually after the legislation of 1964–65, the frontier strategy and the filibuster weapon simply had no further use.

Even though the filibuster had served its purpose in defending segregation, it has nevertheless been invoked, and also implemented, almost continuously in the Senate during the past fifty years since segregation ended. Indeed, it has become a procedural maneuver that seems to be fundamental to the operation of the upper chamber. Rather than a device to obstruct or delay passage of civil rights measures as it was wielded by a minority of southern senators, the filibuster is nowadays threatened, although almost never implemented, as part of the routine of the Senate. And it is deployed by the minority party in order to prevent the party in the majority from enacting most of its proposed legislation. In effect, the filibuster has become a guarantee that the Senate is governed by minority rule. Making matters worse, this power of the minority party extends even to appointments to federal office, such as ambassadors and judges, who are proposed by the majority party when it controls the presidency. Thus, the minority party can, if it acts as a unit, frustrate the administration's ability to govern as well as Congress's ability to legislate.

The irony of this situation is that in 1975 the centerpiece of the Senate's effort to reform its procedures was a change in the rules of the filibuster. In order to make it easier to end a filibuster and thereby reduce its ability to obstruct legislation, the number of votes needed to shut off debate was reduced from sixty-seven (two-thirds of the Senate's one hundred members) to sixty (three-fifths of the members). Many senators had wanted to require just a simple majority (51 percent) to end debate. But this reform was rejected, mainly on the grounds that the requirement of a supermajority to end the Senate's sacred ritual of "continuous debate" was a cherished safeguard of minority rights that should not be jettisoned.

Despite this much-heralded reform of the filibuster, the number of cloture motions has increased exponentially ever since. Before 1975, cloture motions to end a filibuster numbered fewer than ten during each Congress, i.e, every two years. Therefore, in the years when the filibusters were being used to delay or defeat civil rights measures, the procedure was employed quite sparingly. But in 1993–94, for example, there were eighty cloture motions and in 2007–08 as many as 139. In the Congresses since 2000, an average of one cloture motion each week has become normal. Remarkably, in the 111th Congress, elected in 2008 along with President Obama, the rate climbed rapidly to about two per week.[9]

This extraordinary state of affairs has arisen for several reasons. First, the 1975 reduction from 67 to 60 of the number of votes needed to pass a motion to cut off debate has made a filibuster seem less threatening because it is easier to stop and requires just nine more votes than a simple majority of 51. In effect, senators now consider the filibuster a normal procedure, instead of a bombshell. Moreover, a change in the Senate's rules in the 1970s that permitted the chamber's business to continue during a filibuster, rather than bringing it to a halt, made a filibuster seem less damaging and disruptive.

A second explanation for this massive increase is the complete impunity that the filibustering minority suffers as a consequence of its obstructionist behavior. Rarely does the filibuster have to be actually implemented, with all the upset and inconvenience of unlimited debate and all-night sessions. Just the threat of a filibuster is all that is needed. Rather than struggling to round up the sixty members needed to defeat the threatened filibuster, the majority simply concedes that it will be almost impossible to get them to appear for the vote. Since this process of mobilizing sixty votes may have to be contemplated as often as once or twice a week, the whole exercise becomes increasingly impossible and futile. And so it is abandoned, to the great benefit of the minority that had threatened endless debate but has won without doing anything.

But the primary reason for this sclerosis in the Senate is that the parties are polarized, probably to a greater degree than ever before in the history of the United States. Because of this, the leaders of the minority party are able to impose unity on its members, who in turn are unwilling to break ranks, cooperate with the opposition, and hand the majority a legislative victory. Since the Senate is rarely controlled by a supermajority of sixty, the minority party's prospects of producing stalemate and gridlock are as good as guaranteed. The mere threat of a filibuster is therefore a winning strategy, with no penalty to be paid for obstructing the operations of the Senate.

The repercussions of this dysfunctional behavior in the Senate are far-reaching, affecting the entire legislative branch and the presidency as well, not to mention the judiciary when the seating of judges is held up under threat of a filibuster. Regrettably, the filibuster has become a danger to American government and has to be defanged in some way, and very soon. Since it is simply a Senate procedure, the tradition of "continuous debate" could be eliminated altogether. Alternatively, debate could be ended either by a simple majority of 51 or by a reasonable time-limit that could be agreed upon beforehand. Any one of these proposals would seem to be reasonable remedies for a situation that, taken advantage of by both parties whenever they are in the minority, is paralyzing the upper chamber. Unfortunately, any change in the rules of the Senate requires a supermajority, specifically the two-thirds fraction that was retained in the 1975 reform. And therein lies the final catch of Rule

22! But the situation has become sufficiently serious in 2011 that action to end minority rule and the internal veto in the Senate has to be taken if order and efficacy are to return to the nation's central government.

The renewed power of the filibuster as a weapon of minority obstructionism is ironic. Of all the features of the southern political tradition, the filibuster and its related frontier mentality and strategy had no reason to persist after the racial order they were employed to defend had been eliminated. By contrast, it took time to dismantle and replace the others. Yet the filibuster which, more than anything else in American government, was the talisman, the symbol, of southern resistance, remains as an instrument to protect minorities. But now this southern weapon protects minority parties and promotes minority rule. Richard Russell and the southern segregationists would be amazed to see how enormously potent their trusty instrument has become. For Senator Calhoun of South Carolina, the present-day filibuster would seem like a dream come true. So much less cumbersome than nullification and the dual presidency that he proposed for protecting the South and its system of slavery. And so much more successful in tying up the U.S. government in knots!

Notes

1. THE ONE-PARTY PARADIGM

1. C. Vann Woodward, "The Search for Southern Identity," *Virginia Quarterly Review* 34 (Summer 1958): 321–38; Ulrich B. Phillips, "The Central Theme of Southern History," *American Historical Review* 34 (October 1928): 30–43.

2. Richard Hofstadter, *The American Political Tradition and the Men Who Made It* (New York: Alfred A. Knopf, 1948), viii.

3. Charles S. Sydnor, *The Development of Southern Sectionalism, 1819–1848* (Baton Rouge: LSU Press, 1948), 316.

4. Earl and Merle Black, *The Rise of Southern Republicans* (Cambridge, Mass.: Harvard University Press, 2002), 404.

5. James H. Broussard, *The Southern Federalists, 1800–1816* (Baton Rouge: LSU Press, 1978), 83.

6. Van Buren's plan and his initiatives toward implementing it are discussed in Robert V. Remini, *Martin Van Buren and the Making of the Democratic Party* (New York: Columbia University Press, 1959), 130–33.

7. Jackson's overwhelming victories in the South in the presidential elections of 1828 and 1832 are discussed in Charles S. Sydnor, *The Development of Southern Sectionalism, 1819–1848* (Baton Rouge: LSU Press, 1948), 193–94, 205–06.

8. Alexander H. Stephens, "Cornerstone Speech," Savannah, Ga., 21 March 1861, in Henry Cleveland, *Alexander H. Stephens, in Public and Private: With Letters and Speeches, Before, During, and Since the War* (Philadelphia, 1866), 717–29 (text of entire speech).

9. Thomas B. Alexander and Richard E. Beringer, *Anatomy of the Confederate Congress* (Nashville: Vanderbilt University Press, 1972), 332.

10. *Charleston Mercury,* editorial, 12 December 1867.

11. Quoted in John Hope Franklin, *Reconstruction: After the Civil War* (Chicago: University of Chicago Press, 1961), 105.

12. John B. Hubbard's report is quoted and discussed in Richard Zuczek, *State of Rebellion: Reconstruction in South Carolina* (Columbia: University of South Carolina Press, 1996), 81.

13. Drew's comment is in C. Vann Woodward, *Origins of the New South, 1877–1913* (Baton Rouge: LSU Press, 1951), 58.

14. Calhoon's statement is in Michael Perman, *Struggle for Mastery: Disfranchisement in the South, 1888–1908* (Chapel Hill: University of North Carolina Press, 2001), 70.

15. For the history of disfranchisement and the creation of the white primary, see Perman, *Struggle for Mastery.*

16. V. O. Key, Jr., *Southern Politics in State and Nation* (New York: Alfred A. Knopf, 1949), 447.

17. Ibid., 346, 16.

2. THE FRONTIER AND FILIBUSTER DEFENSE: ORIGINS AND DEVELOPMENT

1. Kenneth Rayner, speech to North Carolina assembly, 8 December 1856, in Gregg Cantrell, *Kenneth and John B. Rayner and the Limits of Southern Dissent* (Urbana: University of Illinois Press, 1993), 116.

2. Don E. Fehrenbacher, *The Slaveholding Republic* (New York: Oxford University Press, 2001), chaps. 3 and 4.

3. Don E. Fehrenbacher, *Sectional Crisis and Southern Constitutionalism* (Baton Rouge: LSU Press, 1995), 15, 17, 18.

4. John Randolph, House speech on the General Survey bill, January 1824, quoted in John Lauritz Larson, *Internal Improvement: National Public Works and the Promise of Popular Government in the Early United States* (Chapel Hill: University of North Carolina Press, 2001), 143.

5. These phrases come from Calhoun's speech on Internal Improvements, 4 February 1817, in *Papers of John C. Calhoun,* ed. Robert Meriwether, Edwin W. Hemphill, and Clyde N. Wilson (Columbia, S.C.: University of South Carolina Press, 1959–2003), 1:401.

6. John Quincy Adams to Charles W. Upham, 2 February 1837, in *The Selected Writings of John Quincy Adams,* ed. Adrienne Koch and William Peden (1946; Westport, Conn.: Greenwood, 1981), 389.

7. Calhoun to Daniel Webster, 22 March 1838, in *Papers of John C. Calhoun,* 14:24.

8. Calhoun, Senate speech on the Subtreasury bill, 18 September 1837, *Papers of John C. Calhoun,* 13:569–70.

9. Hammond, speech in the House, 18 December 1835, in William Lee Miller, *Arguing about Slavery* (New York: Alfred A. Knopf, 1996), 33.

10. Calhoun, speech in the Senate, 7 January 1836, in *Papers of John C. Calhoun,* 13:22.

11. Ibid.

12. Calhoun, speech in the Senate, 11 March 1836, in *Papers of John C. Calhoun,* 13:111.

13. Don E. Fehrenbacher, *The Dred Scott Case: Its Significance in American Law and Politics* (New York: Oxford University Press, 1978), 122.

14. Calhoun, Senate speech on abolitionist petitions, 9 March 1836, in *Papers of John C. Calhoun,* 13:105.

15. John P. King, speech in the Senate, quoted in Merrill D. Peterson, *The Great Triumvirate: Webster, Clay, and Calhoun* (New York: Oxford University Press, 1987), 260.

16. See George C. Rable, "The South and the Politics of Antilynching Legislation, 1920–1940," *Journal of Southern History* 51 (May 1985): 201–20. The terms of the Dyer bill are described on pp. 203–04.

17. William W. Larson, speech in the House, 18 January 1922, 67th Cong., 2d sess., *Congressional Record* 62, pt. 2:1376.

18. Hatton W. Sumners, speech in the House, 4 January 1922, 67th Cong., 2d sess., *Congressional Record* 62, pt. 1:798, 801.

19. Fred H. Dominick, speech in the House, 4 January 1922, 67th Cong., 2d sess., *Congressional Record* 62, pt. 2:1345.

20. James Byrnes, speech in the House, 19 December 1921, 67th Cong., 2d sess., *Congressional Record* 62, pt. 1:543, 544.

21. Sumners, speech in the House, 4 January 1922, 67th Cong., 2d sess., *Congressional Record* 62, pt. 1:798.

22. Patrick H. Drewry, speech in the House, 17 January 1922, 67th Cong., 2d sess., *Congressional Record* 62, pt. 2:1307.

23. Finis J. Garrett, speech in the House, 19 December 1921, 67th Cong., 2d sess., *Congressional Record* 62, pt. 1:548.

24. John J. McSwain, speech in the House, 19 December 1921, 67th Cong., 2d sess., *Congressional Record* 62, pt. 1:552.

25. Edgar C. Ellis, speech in the House, 18 January 1922, 67th Cong., 2d sess., *Congressional Record* 62, pt. 2:1347, 1348.

26. Ibid.

27. Walter E. Edge, speech in the Senate, 28 November 1922, 67th Cong., 3d sess., *Congressional Record* 63, proceedings and index 333.

28. John N. Sandlin, speech in the House, 18 January 1922, 67th Cong., 3d sess., *Congressional Record* 62, pt. 2:1358. Rankin's remark was offered in a speech the next day (p. 1427).

29. Sumners, speech in the House, 26 January 1922, 67th Cong., 2d sess., *Congressional Record* 62, pt. 2:1786.

30. Sumners, speech in the House, 4 January 1922, 67th Cong., 2d sess., *Congressional Record* 62, pt. 1:803.

31. James P. Woods, speech in the House, 18 January 1922, 67th Cong., 2d sess., *Congressional Record* 62, pt. 2:1365.

32. Hallett S. Ward, speech in the House, 17 January 1922, 67th Cong., 2d sess., *Congressional Record* 62, pt. 2:1297.

33. Oscar W. Underwood, speech in the Senate, 28 November 1922, 67th Cong., 3d sess., *Congressional Record* 63, proceedings and index, 332. The description of the measure as a "force bill" arose from the precedent of the three "force bills" of 1870–71 that gave the federal government authority to supervise elections in the South and take action against the employment of violence by the Ku Klux Klan. These Reconstruction-era laws that were intended to enforce the Fifteenth Amendment had been described pejoratively as "force bills" by their southern opponents. More recently, the federal elections bill of 1890, often called the "Lodge bill" after its sponsor in the House, Henry Cabot Lodge, was also derided as a "force bill."

34. Underwood, speech, 29 November 1922, ibid., 390, 391.

35. Henry Cabot Lodge, speech in the Senate, 4 December 1922, 67th Cong., 3d sess., *Congressional Record* 63, proceedings and index, 430.

36. Underwood, speech in the Senate, 29 November 1922, 67th Cong., 3d sess., *Congressional Record* 63, proceedings and index, 392.

37. Rable, "The South and the Politics of Antilynching," 208–12.

38. Ibid., 213–17; J. Joseph Huthmacher, *Senator Robert F. Wagner and the Rise of Urban Liberalism* (New York: Atheneum, 1968), 238–43; also 171–74, for the earlier Costigan-Wagner bill.

39. Richard B. Russell, speech in the Senate, 26 January 1938, 75th Cong., 3d sess., *Congressional Record* 83, pt. 1:1101, 1100.

3. THE FRONTIER AND FILIBUSTER DEFENSE: FINAL PHASE

1. William Colmer, speech in the House, 12 October 1942, 77th Cong., 2d sess., *Congressional Record* 88, pt. 6:8167.

2. Theodore Bilbo, speech in the Senate, 19 November 1942, 77th Cong., 2d sess., *Congressional Record* 88, pt. 6:8958.

3. These three cloture votes are analyzed in Steven F. Lawson, *Black Ballots: Voting Rights in the South, 1944–1969* (New York: Columbia University Press, 1976), 79–80.

4. Russell's observation, made in private on 5 March 1949, is in Keith M. Finley, *Delaying the Dream: Southern Senators and the Fight against Civil Rights, 1938–1965* (Baton Rouge: LSU Press, 2008), 112.

5. Johnston's comment of 29 January 1949, also in private correspondence, is ibid., 113.

6. The account that follows covers the late 1940s and the 1950s and it owes a great deal to Keith M. Finley's *Delaying the Dream.* This fine study is the only scholarly treatment of the final phase of the South's fight against the threat of civil rights legislation. It proved impossible to tell the story of the region's last twenty years of reliance on the frontier and filibuster defense without drawing on Finley's authoritative examination of the Southern Caucus's actions in the Senate.

7. This maneuver by the Southern Caucus led by Russell is described and analyzed ibid., 114–21.

8. Etheridge's assurances can be found in George B. Tindall, *The Emergence of the New South, 1913–1945* (Baton Rouge: LSU Press, 1967), 714.

9. Byrd's statement in a Senate speech on 1 February 1946 is in Finley, *Delaying the Dream,* 89.

10. Ervin's assessment of Russell is from an oral interview in the Russell Library, located in Athens, Georgia, quoted in Robert A. Caro, *The Years of Lyndon Johnson: Master of the Senate* (New York: Alfred A. Knopf, 2002), 186.

11. Russell to W. B. Crawford, 30 March 1949, Russell MSS, quoted in Finley, *Delaying the Dream,* 122.

12. See Finley, *Delaying the Dream,* chap. 2.

13. Russell's declamation is quoted in Robert Mann, *The Walls of Jericho: Lyndon Johnson, Hubert Humphrey, Richard Russell, and the Struggle for Civil Rights* (New York: Harcourt, Brace, 1996), 405.

14. Robert Mann discusses this option ibid., 429–30.

15. Russell's Senate speech just before the final vote on the civil rights bill, 19 June 1964, in Finley, *Delaying the Dream,* 277.

4. THE OVER-REPRESENTATION MECHANISM

1. John C. Calhoun, speech in the Senate, 12 February 1836, in *Papers of John C. Calhoun,* 13:73.

2. James H. Hammond, speech in the House, 4 March 1858, in *Congressional Globe,* 35th Cong., 1st sess., new series, 61, pt. 1:962.

3. Alexander H. Stephens, speech to Georgia secession convention, January 1861, in Jesse T. Carpenter, *The South as a Conscious Minority, 1789–1861: A Study in Political Thought* (1930; Gloucester, Mass.: Peter Smith, 1963), 180–81.

4. See Leonard Richards, *The Slave Power: The Free North and Southern Domination, 1780–1860* (Baton Rouge: LSU Press, 2000), 9–10, notes 13, 15.

5. Eric Foner, *Free Soil, Free Labor, Free Men: The Ideology of the Republican Party before the Civil War* (1970; rev. ed., New York: Oxford University Press, 1995), 99.

6. See Leonard Richards's calculation in *Slave Power*, 56–57, and graphic on 57.

7. For southerners' influence within the Republican caucus, see Richards, *Slave Power*, 58–78.

8. Don E. Fehrenbacher, *The Slaveholding Republic: An Account of the United States Government's Relations to Slavery* (New York: Oxford University Press, 2001), 29–33, and chap. 2.

9. See Richards, *Slave Power*, chap. 2.

10. For discussion of the "three-fifths clause," see Fehrenbacher, *Slaveholding Republic*, chap. 2, and Richards, *Slave Power*, chap. 2. See also Garry Wills, *"Negro President": Jefferson and the Slave Power* (New York: Houghton Mifflin, 2003), chaps. 3–6.

11. Richards, *The Life and Times of Congressman John Quincy Adams* (New York: Oxford University Press, 1986), 10.

12. Ibid., 15.

13. Richards, *Slave Power*, 88–91.

14. Ibid., 48.

15. David P. Currie, *The Constitution in Congress: Democrats and Whigs, 1829–1861* (Chicago: University of Chicago Press, 2005), 278.

16. Quoted in David M. Potter's 1968 Fleming Lectures, published as *The South and the Concurrent Majority* (Baton Rouge: LSU Press, 1968), 24.

17. For specifics on the southern Democrats' position and influence in the Democratic Party during the 1850s, see David M. Potter, *The Impending Crisis, 1848–1861* (New York: Harper and Row, 1976), 326.

18. Garfield, quoted in Potter, *The South and the Concurrent Majority*, 33–34.

19. Marlin Olmsted, speech in the House, 3 January 1901, 56th Cong., 2d sess., *Congressional Record* 34, pt. 1:608.

20. Booker T. Washington to President Theodore Roosevelt, 29 July 1904, in *The Booker T. Washington Papers*, ed. Louis R. Harlan and Raymond Smock (Urbana: University of Illinois Press, 1972–1989), 8:35.

21. For the specifics of the campaign to punish the authors of disfranchisement by reducing southern representation in the House, see Michael Perman, *Struggle for Mastery: Disfranchisement in the South, 1888–1908* (Chapel Hill: University of North Carolina Press, 2001), chap. 11.

22. John Sharp Williams, speech in the House, 4 January 1901, 56th Cong., 2d sess., *Congressional Record* 34, pt. 1:558.

23. See Perman, *Struggle for Mastery*, chap. 6.

24. V. O. Key, Jr., *Southern Politics in State and Nation* (New York: Alfred A. Knopf, 1949), 315.

25. See Potter, *The South and the Concurrent Majority*, 40–44.

26. In the 1910s, when the Democrats controlled Congress during Wilson's presidency, the southern Democrats also controlled the congressional committees. As in the 1930s when Franklin Roosevelt was president, they had been extremely influential in getting Wilson's agenda enacted and also in determining its content and priorities. For a discussion of the South's role in the Wilson administration, see George B. Tindall, *The Emergence of the New South, 1913–1945* (Baton Rouge: LSU Press, 1967), chaps. 1–5, and Elizabeth Sanders, *Roots of Reform: Framers, Workers, and the American State, 1877–1917* (Chicago: University of Chicago Press, 1999), especially part II, "The Agrarian Statist Agenda."

27. Paul H. Douglas, *In the Fullness of Time: The Memoirs of Paul H. Douglas* (New York: Harcourt, Brace, 1972), 206–07.

28. Ibid., 202.

29. Ibid., 204.

30. William S. White, *Citadel: The Story of the U.S. Senate* (New York: Harper and Row, 1956), 68.

5. THE DISMANTLING OF THE SOUTHERN POLITICAL TRADITION

1. Lyndon Johnson's prediction is reported in Joseph Califano, *The Triumph and Tragedy of Lyndon Johnson: The White House Years* (New York: Simon and Schuster, 1991), 55.

2. Earl and Merle Black, *The Rise of Southern Republicans* (Cambridge, Mass.: Harvard University Press, 2002), chap. 5.

3. Stephen Ansolabehere and James M. Snyder, Jr., *The End of Inequality: One Person, One Vote, and the Transformation of American Politics* (New York: W. W. Norton, 2008), 188.

4. This issue is discussed succinctly by David Lublin in *The Republican South: Democratization and Partisan Change* (Princeton, N.J.: Princeton University Press, 2004), 99–115; Ansolabehere and Snyder in *The End of Equality*, 258–62; and Bernard Grofman and Lisa Handley in "Estimating the Impact of Voting Rights–Related Districting on Democratic Strength in the U.S. House of Representatives," in *Race and Redistricting in the 1990s*, ed. Bernard Grofman (New York: Agathon Press, 1998), 51–65. See also a collection of essays edited by David A. Bositis entitled *Voting Rights and Minority Representation: Redistricting, 1992–2002* (Lanham, Md.: University Press of America, 2006), esp. chaps. 3 (by Bositis) and 5 (by Lublin).

5. For the origins of the campaign to reform Congress, see Julian E. Zelizer, *On Capitol Hill: The Struggle to Reform Congress and Its Consequences, 1948–2000* (New York: Cambridge University Press, 2004), chap. 6.

6. See Zelizer, *On Capitol Hill,* chaps. 6 and 7.

7. For the culmination of the campaign to reform Congress, see Zelizer, *On Capitol Hill,* chaps. 8 and 9.

8. For the filibuster in the nineteenth century, see Gregory J. Wawro and Eric Schickler, *Filibuster: Obstruction and Lawmaking in the U.S. Senate* (Princeton, N.J.: Princeton University Press, 2006), chaps. 1–7.

9. An excellent analysis and critique of the filibuster crisis in the Senate is Michael Tomasky, "The Specter Haunting the Senate," *New York Review of Books,* 30 September 2010, 22, 24, 26. Also of interest is George Packer, "The Empty Chamber: Is the Senate Beyond Hope?" *New Yorker,* 9 August 2010, 38–51.

Index

Index

Index